Build Your First Website with Flash MX

Keran McKenzie
Todd Yard

Build Your First Website with Flash MX

© 2002 friends of ED

First Printed December 2002

Photographs © Ruth McKenzie

Trademark Acknowledgements

Published by friends of ED

30-32 Lincoln Road, Olton, Birmingham.
B27 6PA. UK.
Printed in USA

ISBN 1-904344-12-7

Credits

Authors
Keran McKenzie
Todd Yard

Additional Material
Sally Cruikshank
Matt Knight

Reviewers
Alexandra Blackburn
Sally Cruikshank
Vibha Roy
Mike Sloan
Jessica Strobel

Proof Reader
Helena Sharman

Managing Editor
Chris Hindley

Commissioning Editor
Andrew Tracey

Technical Editors
Victoria Blackburn
Dan Britton
Libby Hayward
Matt Knight

Author Agent
Chris Matterface

Project Manager
Simon Brand

Graphic Editor
Matt Clark

Indexer
Simon Collins

Cover and Design
Matt Clark
Katy Freer

Initial Concept Work
Dan Squier

Keran McKenzie

Keran has been involved in web development since late 1994. In 1997 he became interested in an application called FutureSplash, which would become Flash.

Keran has been working with Flash ever since, and now runs the web solutions agency Kiwi Interactive. He is founder and webmaster of Studiowhiz.com, and co-founder and webmaster at flashcomponent.com.

I'd like to thank my friends at Studiowhiz.com who assisted with testing, and my wife, who not only put up with the long hours of work, but also provided the photography for the site. Her support means everything to me.

Todd Yard

After studying theatre in London, then working for several years as an actor in the US, Todd was introduced to Flash in 2000. He was quickly taken by how it allowed for both stunning creativity and programmatic logic - a truly left-brain, right-brain approach to production - and has not looked back.

He now works as Creative Director for Daedalus Media in New York City, which specializes in the creation of Flash-based corporate presentations, primarily for clients in the investment banking industry. His more frivolous work and experimentation can be found at his personal site, www.27Bobs.com.

TABLE OF CONTENTS

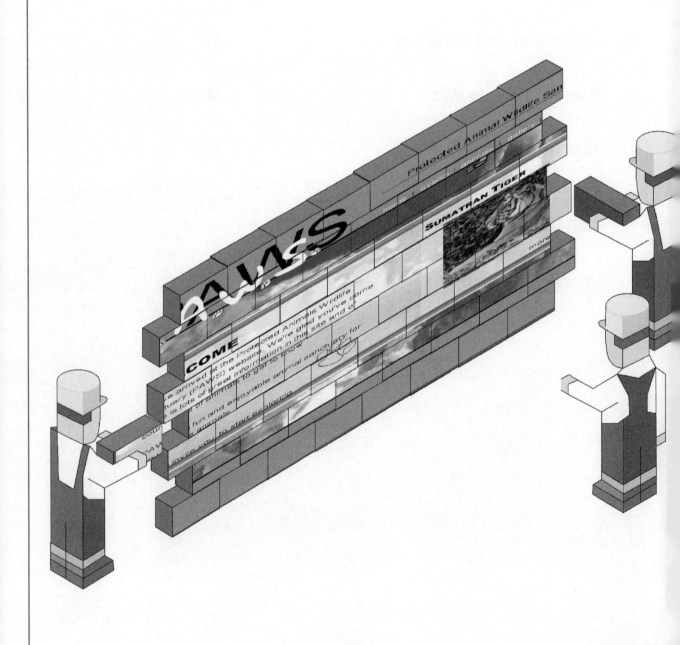

Welcome to **Build Your First Website with Flash MX**. Why would you want to use Flash to build your website? Well, Flash is used to make lots of stunning looking interactive sites on the web, but it's easy to use, and this book will show you just how simple it is to learn.

> *For the first time it's incredibly **easy** to make interactive motion graphics for the web.*

We will teach you the wonders of Flash through simple-to-follow, step-by-step-examples which build up to a final, impressive website

What you'll need

The beauty of this book is that you should already have everything you need. Obviously you'll need a computer, either a Mac or a PC running Windows, which, if you're interested in web design, you'll probably have already.

You'll need Flash MX running on your machine. If you already have a full version of the software then great. If not, you'll need to install the fully-functional trial version of Flash MX which we've included on the CD at the back of the book. This will act in exactly the same way as the full version, but only for 30 days from the time you install it. This should be plenty of time for you to work your way through the book, get to familiarize yourself with Flash MX, and be in a position to decide (as we're sure you will) that you want to continue with the software in the future. At this point you can go and buy the full version, safe in the knowledge that you know you'll like it and will be able to use it to create fantastic-looking sites.

As the book is a series of examples, you'll be creating files as you go along. If, at any point, you're not getting the results you expect, or feel you may have gone wrong in following the steps somewhere, you'll be able to use the source files on the CD to check exactly where you're supposed to be.

Also on the CD you'll find trial versions of other great Macromedia products. There's Dreamweaver MX, which you can use to make more standard, less interactive websites, along with Freehand 10 and Fireworks MX, which you can use to create graphics to include in your designs.

Setting things up

I don't know about you but I like to see results fast, and I like to have something to work towards.

In order to do this, we're going to work on a project throughout the book. This project will be a website for a nature reserve, which wants a cutting edge site to boost visitor figures, a news page, an events page that they can update, animal content pages the local schoolchildren can use and some details about the company.

Take a look at the picture to have a look at what we'll have created by the end of the book.

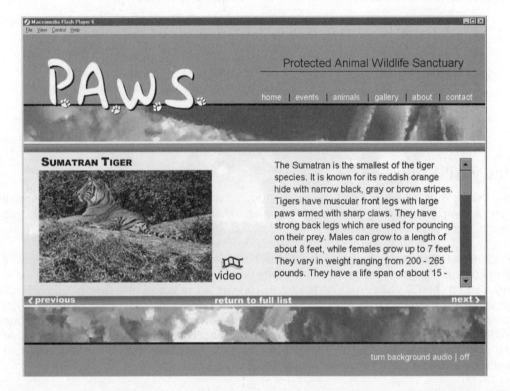

Target audience is internet marketing speak for "who do you want to visit your site?". We've sat down with the people at the nature reserve and asked them who they think their target audience is. They think that that most visitors are going to be in the 24 to 55 age bracket, and enjoy animals. They don't have any statistics on their level of technology understanding but think most have a computer at home.

Let's say that most of these people buy their computer from a store – allowing us to say that the majority of the target audience would be...

- Using Microsoft Windows ME or XP Home
- Using Internet Explorer 6
- Running their 15" monitor at 800x600 resolution
- Use 56k dial up modem for internet
- Have 1 email address

We know that our users have displays running at 800x600 pixels, but if we allow for the usual browser tool bars and so on, we're probably left with something more like 750x500 pixels, so we're going to go for 640x480 to make sure we fit the screen.

1. Go ahead and open Flash. When you've started up Flash for the first time, it should have opened a blank Flash file for you (it'll say something like Untitled-1 at the top of the screen). If this hasn't happened, select `File > New` to give yourself a new file.

2. You should see something similar to the following picture. The entire area is known as the **work area**, and the white area in the middle is the **stage**. (You can turn the work area off `View > Work area` and this puts the top left of the stage in the top left of the stage window). If we think about our Flash work as being like a play, then actors can only be seen when they are standing on the stage. If they are on the work area they can be talked to, and they can influence the actors on the stage but they are not seen.

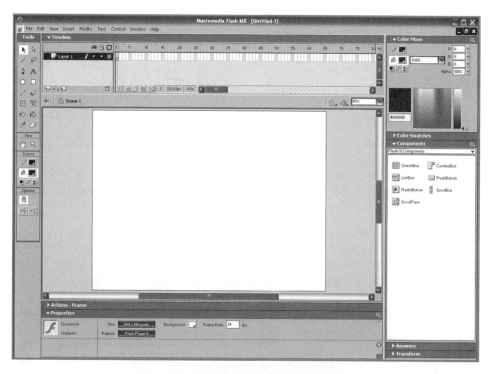

3. As we'll be discovering throughout the book, you can create a lot of different items in Flash. All of these have attributes that can be changed – for a graphic, you could change the color, or the size; for text, you could change the font; and so on. These attributes are called **Properties**. There's a specially designed bar to allow you to select something and then alter its properties. This bar is called the **Property inspector** and this should be at the bottom of your screen, looking like the picture below. If you can't see it, you need to go to `Window > Properties`. Get used to this bar, it will be your loyal and trusty sidekick in your Flash adventures.

4. At the moment, you've not created anything in your Flash movie that can be selected, so the Property inspector gives you the **properties** for the **stage**. The defaults for these are a width of 550 pixels and a height of 400 pixels, a Frame rate of 12, a background color of white, and a Publish: setting of Flash Player 6. What does this all mean? Well, the size and background colors you can probably work out for yourselves! Setting the Background color means that every part of your Flash movie will have that color as a background, so if you're not going to use white, make sure that you're selecting a color you don't mind seeing a lot of.

5. We'll be learning more about Frames in the next chapter, but the Frame rate sets how fast you want Flash to run through your movie – we want things to move a bit faster than the default, so change this from 12 to 24. The Publish: setting allows us to tell Flash to save our Flash MX files so that people with the Flash 5 plug-in can see them. We're not going to worry about this here: a lot of people have the MX plug-in, and this would mean that we couldn't use some of Flash MX's best features (like video, for example).

> These settings are not fixed – we can come back and alter them anytime we like.

At the moment, unless you're lucky enough to have one of those huge monitors that necessitate an extra desk, your Flash screen is probably looking a little crowded. The nice thing about Flash is that the interface is totally customizable: you can move everything around so that you're completely comfortable. Each of the panels on your screen can be moved around, minimized/maximized, docked (so that it sits underneath another panel), or closed down. As you can see from the pictures, clicking on the white arrow will minimize/maximize, clicking and holding on the black dots to the left of the arrow will allow you to move the panel around (drop it on another panel to dock), and right-clicking will give you some options, including closing the panel. Have a play around to get used to things.

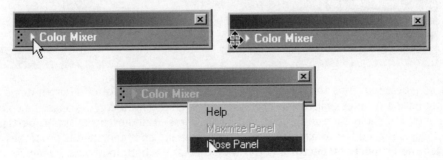

I'd suggest you leave the **Tools** panel (probably on the left of your screen), the **Timeline** panel (probably at the top of your screen), and the previously discussed **Property inspector** panel as we're going to be using them all fairly soon. You can get rid of the rest, though – you can always get them (or any other window) back at any time by selecting them from the Window menu.

Macs/PCs

You can use Flash MX on both Macs and PCs. For the purposes of consistency, we've used PC screenshots throughout the book, but things should look pretty much the same if you're using a Mac.

To keep the book as easy to read as possible, we've used PC commands as a default, so that every time you come across a mouse command you don't have to read something long-winded like, 'right-click on the PC or CTRL-click on the Mac'.

When we just say 'click' we mean *left*-click on the PC or simply *click* on the Mac. The common substitute commands are:

PC	Mac
Right-click	CTRL-click
CTRL-click	APPLE-click
CTRL-Z (to undo)	APPLE-Z
CTRL-ENTER	APPLE-ENTER

Support

All books from friends of ED aim to be easy to follow and error-free. However, if you do run into problems, don't hesitate to get in touch – our support is fast, friendly, and free.

This book has a dedicated discussion forum at www.buildyourfirst.com, where you can ask for advice on particular problems, show us what you've been able to create, or discuss any other Flash-related topics. Please drop by and let us know how it's going – the more we hear from you, the more we can make sure that we produce the right books for you.

You can also reach us by emailing support@friendsofED.com, quoting the last four digits of the ISBN in the subject of the e-mail (that's 4127 for those of you too lazy to turn over to the back cover). If you're having technical problems with a specific file that you've created from an exercise, it can sometimes help to include a copy of that file with your mail.

Even if our dedicated support team is unable to solve your problem immediately, your queries will be passed onto the people who put the book together - the editors and authors - to solve. All foED authors help with the support on their books, and will either directly mail people with answers, or (more usually) send their response to an editor to pass on.

We'd love to hear from you, whether it's to request future books, ask about friends of ED, or tell us about the sites you went on to create after you read this book.

To tell us a bit about yourself and make comments about the book, why not fill out the reply card at the back and send it to us!

For news, more books, sample chapters, downloads, author interviews and more, send your browser to www.friendsofED.com.

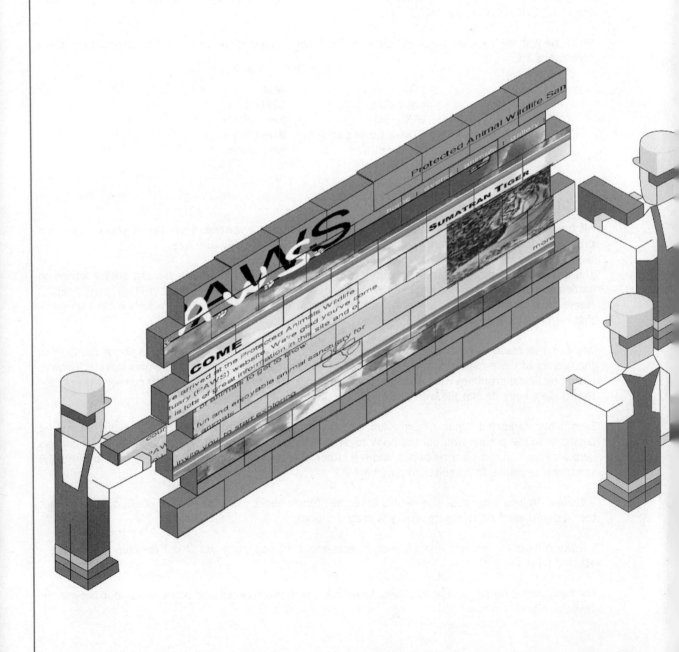

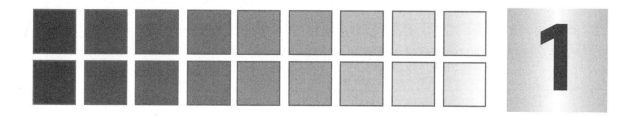

Creating Simple Graphics

Flash allows you to create graphical elements in a variety of ways. We are going to start by exploring the **drawing tools**.

1. Open Flash, and save the file as random_effects.fla; we'll use this file to create some of our artwork. The drawing tools that we'll be using all come from the **Tools panel**, as pictured. We'll be using these as we go along, but if you're looking for something in particular, then:

- The **Tools** section at the top contains all the drawing and manipulation options, for drawing, adding text, and altering or moving the drawings and text.

- The **View** section allows you to change the position of the stage on the screen, and to zoom in and out.

- The **Colors** section allows you to set and change the colors you're using.

- In the **Options** section, you can set options for the tool you've selected from above. For example, if you select the Pencil tool, you will notice that you can select from three modes – Straighten, Smooth, and Ink (try drawing on the stage to see the difference).

> *With the Zoom button (the magnifying glass icon under View), hold down the ALT key to swap between zoom in or zoom out. You can also double-click the button to jump back to 100%.*

2. We're going to start by drawing a leaf, which we'll be using as an element in our site. Select the **Line** tool from the Tools panel. As you can see from the picture, we want to start with a horizontal line towards the bottom of the stage. To do this, click where you want the line to start, hold the mouse button down, and release it where you want the line to end. If you want a perfectly horizontal or vertical line, hold the SHIFT key down while you do this.

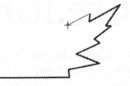

3. If you're having problems getting your lines right at this stage, then select the Zoom tool from the View section of the Tools panel. When you've selected the Zoom tool, you'll see that the Options section at the bottom of the panel allows you to choose whether to zoom in (enlarge) or out (reduce). Choose the enlarge option, and click once on your leaf.

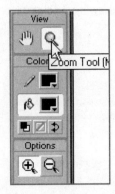

4. The following image shows the stages to create the base leaf shape – we're going to modify this in a moment, so don't worry about the way it looks. Just repeat the drag, release, drag, release till you have a very square and "sharp" looking leaf. To create a more natural and life-like leaf, don't put the top point in the exact center – the one shown leans slightly to the right.

5. If you're having trouble getting the lines to connect, there's a **Snap to Objects** tool to help you, which will help join your lines to whatever other line is nearest. If you choose the Arrow tool at the top left of the Tools

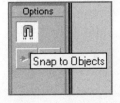

panel, you'll see a little magnet-like icon at the bottom of the Tools menu in the Options section (as shown). Select this to turn Snap to Objects on.

6. OK, by now you've probably made a mistake and drawn a line somewhere you don't want to. You could use Edit > Undo to undo whatever you've just done, but what we really need is a little more control. Select the **Arrow** tool from the top left of the Tools panel.

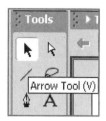

7. On the stage, identify the part of the line you want to delete. If you've got a problem clearly spotting where this starts and ends, Zoom in (use the button in the View section of the Tools panel, or View > Zoom). Click, and hold your mouse button down, and drag a box around the part you want to remove. When you let go, the box will disappear, but look carefully, and you'll see that the part of your line that you surrounded with a box is highlighted. When you draw your box, be careful to start a little way away from your line (as pictured) – if you click on your line, then the whole line will be highlighted. Press DELETE, and the highlighted section of your line will disappear.

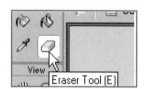

8. There is also an **Eraser** tool. Click on the tool and then simply click and drag to rub out items. The Eraser tool also has some options. Under the Options panel, open the drop-down menu to see a list of potential shape erasers for you to use.

9

9. All shapes that we create in Flash can con-
sist of a **stroke** and a **fill**. So far, our leaf
has a **stroke** - the line that goes around an
object. Were we to fill the inside of the leaf
with a color, we would be adding a **fill**. In
the Colors section of the Tools panel, you
can pick colors before you draw a shape:
the top color chip is for the stroke and the
bottom one is for the fill. You can set these
colors before you create your objects, or
you can use the Ink Bottle and Paint Bucket
tools to change them afterwards, which is
what we're going to do now.

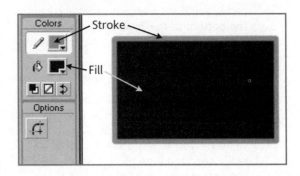

10. Select the **Ink Bottle** tool. Choose a dark
green color by clicking on the stroke color
chip.

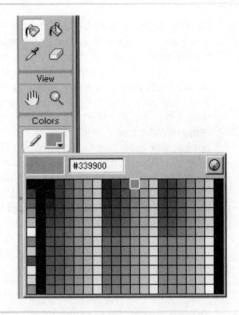

11. Position the inkbottle icon over your leaf
outline, with the end of the "ink" on your
line. Click to color your outline green. This
should color your whole outline the selected green: if not, just use the inkbottle in a
couple more places where the old color
remains.

12. Now choose the **Paint Bucket** tool. This
allows us to add (or change) a fill. Choose a
dark yellow color from the fill color chip.
Position the paint bucket cursor anywhere

in the middle of your leaf, and click to fill it yellow.

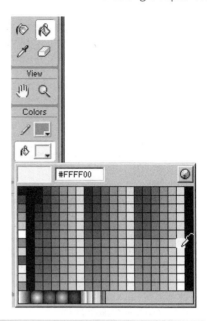

13. There are three small buttons under the fill color. These buttons will affect the fill or the stroke, depending which one you've selected. The first button will turn whichever option you have selected to black, and the other to white to give you a monochrome color scheme. The last button will swap your fill and stroke colors around. The middle button is far more important, and we'll be using it throughout the book, as it removes the fill or the stroke. When we say that we need to draw a strokeless black rectangle, for example, you'll need settings as shown in the screenshot.

14. Now we want to give the leaf a little life - you don't get straight lines like that in nature, so let's add some curves. Make sure that you still have the Arrow tool selected in the Tools panel, and move your cursor towards the bottom line of your leaf until the cursor looks like this:

15. Once your cursor looks like this, click and hold and then move to make the line curved.

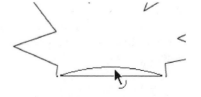

16. Once you've done this, go ahead and make the rest of the lines curved, until you end up with a leaf similar to the one shown:

> *Before you go any further, save your file. We are doing quite a lot here, so save often.*

17. You'll also have noticed that the curved symbol changes to a square one (as pictured) when you get to the end of a line; this allows you to drag the straight lines out. For the stem, select the Line tool again, and add a couple of straight lines to the base, and use this to drag the lines out to the right length, before adding a little natural curve. Don't forget that you'll have to switch to the Line tool to draw the lines and then go back to the Arrow tool to modify them.

18. So far, all the lines we've drawn have been a very standard size, but we can change this too. With the Arrow tool selected, draw a box around your leaf. You'll see that all of the leaf is selected. Hold down the SHIFT key, and click on the fill in the middle of your leaf. This will deselect the fill, making sure that only your stroke (or outline) is selected.

19. If you look in the Property inspector (open it with Windows > Properties if you can't see it), you'll see that you can change stroke and fill colors here, too – it doesn't make any difference whether you do that here or in the Tools panel. We're more interested in the drop-down menu, which sets the thickness of the stroke; and in the drop-down box next to that, which sets the line type. To make the edge of our leaf more natural, set it to 0.75 thickness, and choose an uneven edge, as shown.

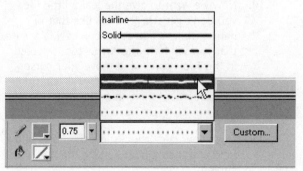

20. One thing we can do is add some variety to all that flat yellow color in the middle of our leaf, to make it look a little more natural. First of all, add some lines to your leaf with the Line tool, with the same stroke settings as we've just used for the edges. Now select all of your leaf – fill and stroke – by selecting the Arrow tool, and drawing a big box around it.

21. Choose the Brush tool, which will allow us to add some natural looking patches of color to our leaf. If you look under Options at the bottom of the Tools panel, you'll see that the Brush tool has some cool options: you can choose to paint over objects, just inside objects, or just behind lines, for example. The one we want is `Paint Selection`, which will only allow us to paint our selection. As we've just selected our leaf, this will only allow us to paint our leaf – no messy edges on the stage.

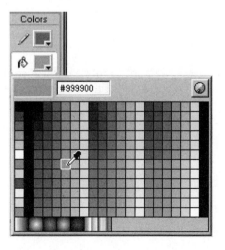

22. Select an olive color from the fill color chip, and a smallish brush shape from the drop-down box in the Options section, and try painting along the sides of your leaf. The brush will only paint inside the leaf, allowing you to add some natural looking tints to the leaf. Add some color inside the leaf as well (try a bit of brown as well, if you're feeling adventurous).

23. The Free Transform tool (just under the
Pencil tool) is very powerful: it wraps the
selected item with three control points per
side and allows you to scale, skew, and
rotate that object. Once again, select all of
our leaf, and choose the Free Transform
tool from the panel. If you hold the cursor
in different places, you should see it change
to allow you to:

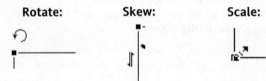

If you hold down the SHIFT key, the transformations take place in
steps. The rotation occurs in 45 degree steps, for example.

24. Here, we want to rotate our leaf so that it's
at an angle. Select the leaf, select the Free
Transform tool, and away you go.

25. Now, we have a leaf on the stage – great. What happens if we want another leaf? Well, we could copy and paste our original to create another one, but Flash has a smarter way of doing things. To save download times, you can turn your leaf into a **Symbol**. This means you can use twelve leaves, but Flash will only have to load the leaf onto a user's machine once. To do this, select all of your leaf, and choose Insert > Convert to Symbol.

26. You should see a box like the one pictured. In Flash, there are three varieties of symbols: movie clips, buttons, and graphics. We'll be taking a look at movie clips and buttons later on, but turn your leaf into a graphic symbol this time around. Each symbol we create must have a unique name, so call this symbol `leaf`.

27. Not only does making our leaf a symbol mean we can create several copies of it, it means that Flash files it for us in the **Library** so that we can find it whenever we need to. Be brave, and delete your leaf from the main stage (select it and press DELETE), so that you're looking at a totally blank stage. Now open up the Library by going to Window > Library. You'll see that our new leaf symbol is there, and that Flash has recognized that it is a graphic symbol.

28. Click on the leaf symbol and drag it out onto the stage. The leaf has returned! Click and drag two further copies of the leaf out onto the stage. You'll notice that there's now a blue box surrounding each of our newly made symbols on the stage. Select one of the symbols. Click once inside the

blue lines, and you'll find that you can hold the mouse button and drag your symbol around the stage.

29. Double-click on one of your new symbols, and you'll notice that the other symbols on the stage are faded out. If you also look at the top-left of your stage, then you'll notice that the name of your symbol is showing. As you've made your graphic into a symbol, you can't just change the way it looks on the stage, because Flash knows that you might have other versions of the symbol that also need to change, so it allows you to **Edit in Place**. This allows you to change your leaf without altering its position on the stage.

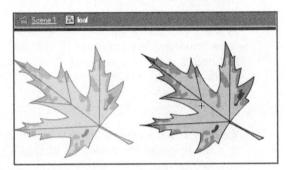

30. Change something on your leaf – the color of the stem, say – and click on the `Scene 1` text at the top-left of your screen to exit Edit Symbol mode and return to the main stage. You'll notice that all three of your leaves have had your change applied to them. Save your file and close it when you've finished – we'll be coming back later to use the leaf in an animation for the site.

Using the Pen tool

The **Pen** tool allows you to draw Bezier curves, which have control handles allowing you to adjust and change the curve. This is a powerful tool that can take some time to get used to, and we're going to start practicing now. Leaves come in all shapes and sizes, so we're going to create a slightly more rounded example than the last exercise.

1. Create a new Flash movie, and save it as `leaf.fla`. Choose the Pen tool from the Tools panel.

2. We're going to start with a simple curve. Roughly where you want the top of your leaf to begin, click and drag your mouse. You'll see a somewhat baffling line created. The center point is the node – where the curve will start from - and the two dark dots are the control handles.

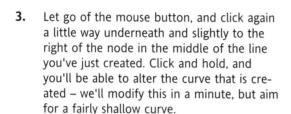

3. Let go of the mouse button, and click again a little way underneath and slightly to the right of the node in the middle of the line you've just created. Click and hold, and you'll be able to alter the curve that is created – we'll modify this in a minute, but aim for a fairly shallow curve.

4. Now do the same again, but to the left this time. Again, don't worry about getting things perfect: this takes a lot of practice, and we'll tidy up our curves in a moment. When you've done this, right-click or hit Esc to stop drawing. If you don't do this, wherever you click next will create another curve, which can be a little irritating!

5. Now, we want to modify our curves a little, so select the Subselection tool from the top right of the Tools panel.

6. Click on the top node, and you'll see a handle appear, which you can select and drag to alter your curve. You can click on any of the three nodes, so do this, and experiment until you've got a reasonably clean, curved line. I'm not pretending this is easy, and it might take a little bit of experimenting to

get right, but the Pen tool can be really useful, so stay with it.

7. This line is going to form the stem of our
    leaf - we're aiming for a leaf like the one
    pictured.

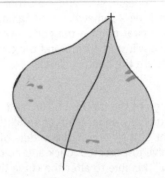

8. To form the rest of the leaf, select the Pen
    tool again. On the top node of our line,
    click and hold down (you may need to do
    this for a few seconds) to create the begin-
    ning of a new curve. Do your best to create
    a rough approximation of the curve along
    the left-hand side. It's probably best to do
    this with two curves: the first is shown:

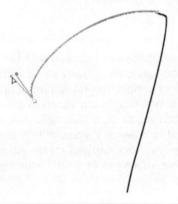

9. No matter how hard you've tried, you'll
    need to play around with this line to get it a
    little bit better. Before you select the
    Subselection tool to do this, try taking the
    Pen tool close to your new line. Click when
    you see a + icon appear next to it, and
    you'll create a new node on your curve that
    you can then alter as usual with the
    Subselection tool. Add a few nodes in places
    where you want to change the curve a little.

10. When you've got something like the line
pictured, move on: the great thing about
leaves is that their edges are irregular and
individual, so there's no reason why your
curves can't be the same. When it comes to
connecting up your lines to each other,
you'll probably want to zoom right in to get
things right.

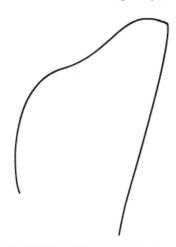

11. Use the same techniques to carry on, and
create something like the shape pictured.
Again, you won't get this first time: you'll
need to add some nodes and experiment a
little.

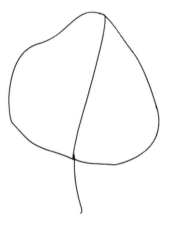

12. When you've got a leaf that you're just
about satisfied with, use the Paint Bucket
tool to add an appropriate fill (I used a dark
yellow color, similar to the last leaf). The
Brush tool we used on the last leaf can be
really useful, but you can also use the Lasso
tool to select an area that you've drawn.
You can then color, move, or delete the
area. Select the Lasso tool from the Tools
panel.

13. On your leaf, select an area by clicking, holding the mouse button down and drawing with the mouse button. Once you release the button, you'll see that the area you've just drawn is highlighted. You can do anything you want with this, but we're just going to color it brown, so choose a dark green from the Fill color chip.

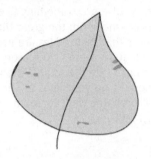

14. When your leaf is finished, go to Edit > Select All to select your leaf, and then choose Insert > Convert to Symbol. Make your leaf into a graphic symbol called `leaf_001`.

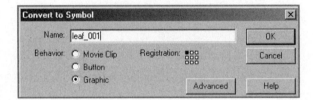

Further steps

We've not made things easy for you: we've dived straight in and shown you how to use the drawing tools that Flash provides. You've already learned the most important skills for producing amazing Flash content.

The tools offer a whole wealth of opportunities for creating content. To carry on using these tools before we continue to the next session, try creating a few more graphics using what you've learned. For example:

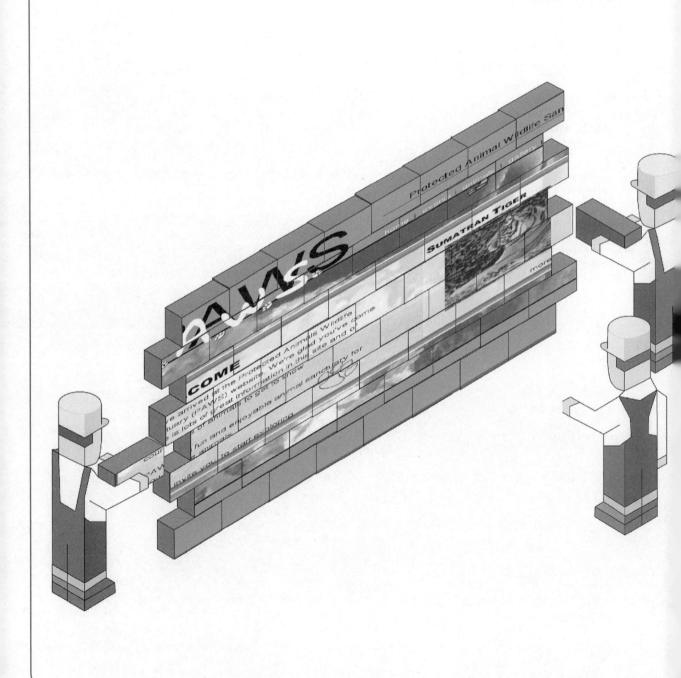

Creating animation

In the last session, we created some static graphics for use in our site. We're now going to move onto what Flash really excels at: adding motion to static graphics. In other words, we're going to **animate** our content.

The **timeline** is probably the most important part of Flash, because it controls what happens over time in a Flash movie. You should be able to see it at the top of your screen (if you can't, Window > Timeline will bring it back).

The timeline is made up of a series of **frames**. Frames are small sections of time that together make up a movie. In the last session, we talked about setting our movies to run at 24fps, meaning that there will be 24 frames played **p**er **s**econd. You can see the frame numbers indicated across the top of the timeline in increments of 5.

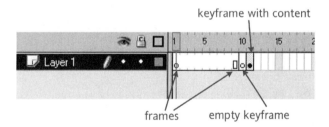

keyframe with content

frames   empty keyframe

When you first open Flash, you'll see that there's only one frame on your timeline, but you can add to this by selecting a place on the timeline and selecting Insert > Frame. If you were to select frame 10, and add a frame there, then Flash will automatically add the frames in between frames 1 and 10.

Adding blank frames is all very well, but they'll always contain exactly the same content as the frame before them. If we want to animate things, then we need to be able to change the appearance of content on different frames. To do this, we use **keyframes**.

If you look at the Insert menu, you'll see that there are two types of keyframes that you can add: standard keyframes and blank keyframes. Adding a standard keyframe will keep the content on the previous frame in it, but any alterations you make to that content will only apply to that keyframe, and any blank frames after it. A blank keyframe will give you a keyframe with no content on it at all.

As you go through the book, always look very carefully at instructions to add keyframes, and make sure you get the right sort. Adding a normal keyframe where you want a blank keyframe will mean that you get content appearing when you don't want it to!

Keyframes are denoted by round circles on the timeline, as shown in the previous graphic. Filled circles indicate that a keyframe holds some content, whilst a hollow circle indicates a blank keyframe that we haven't added anything to yet.

Keyframe animation

Now that we've briefly looked at how the animation is controlled, let's create some keyframe animation so that we can see how this works in practice.

1. Open Flash, if it is not open already, and create a new document. Save it as `butter-fly_animation.fla`. Go to Modify > Document, and set the new movie settings to the same as last time (640x480 and 24fps).

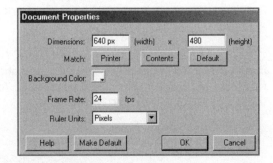

2. Draw the rough shape of a butterfly, as shown (it doesn't need to be perfect). I used the Pen tool; the following images show the steps I went through:

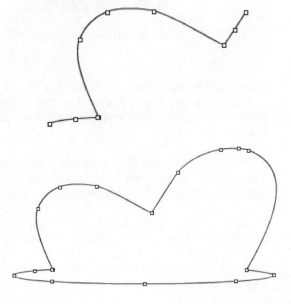

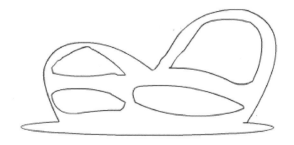

3. Use the Paint Bucket tool to give the butterfly some color. I've selected black as the first fill color, so move the paint bucket cursor to the wing and click to fill, as shown here:

4. Now, choose orange (#FF9900) to fill in the smaller sections.

5. Use the Subselection tool to check that the strokes you have created are **hairline**, as this setting will scale better when we animate the butterfly.

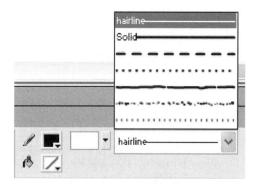

6. Select the Free Transform tool from the Tools panel. Click and drag to draw a box around your new graphic, and use the drag handles on the sides to make your butterfly a little smaller. If you look in your Property inspector, you'll see the size of your butterfly in pixels – I made mine 20 pixels wide and 10 pixels high, so aim for something like that.

> *This will make your butterfly fairly small on the stage, so you might need to use View > Zoom to see your butterfly.*

7. Select the Arrow tool from the Tools panel, and draw a box around your butterfly so that it's selected (you should be able to see that all the lines are highlighted – zoom in if necessary). Now turn it into a graphic symbol by selecting Insert > Convert to Symbol, and call it `butterfly`. Don't forget to select the `Graphic` radio button option, as shown.

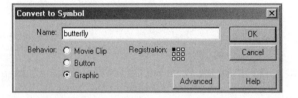

8. Double-click on your new graphic symbol so that you can edit it. Here's where we start to do something different: go to the second frame on your timeline and select it by clicking on it with your mouse. Insert a keyframe by selecting Insert > Keyframe. Now add keyframes to the next six frames, so that you have eight keyframes in a row.

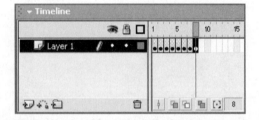

9. Select the second keyframe with your mouse, and select the butterfly picture on the stage. Use the Free Transform tool to make it a bit smaller, as we did earlier. Do the same to the next keyframe and so on, until your butterfly has nearly disappeared on the last keyframe. I've reduced the width of my butterfly in 2 pixel increments and the height in 1 pixel increments, so that my final image is 6x3 pixels in size.

10. Now add six **blank** keyframes, immediately after the eight we already have. Select the seventh frame and go to Edit > Copy. Select the ninth frame, and select Edit > Paste in Place. Copy and paste the sixth frame into

the tenth frame, the fifth into the eleventh, and so on, until you finish by copying the second frame into the fourteenth frame.

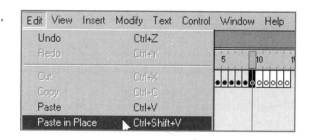

11. What are we doing here? Well, we're creating a **loop**. We've just made the butterfly get smaller and then bigger again. This will loop perfectly, as the last frame merges into the first one perfectly, and Flash will go back to the beginning of the timeline and start again unless told otherwise. If you grab hold of the red block just above your timeline (the official name for this is the **playhead**), and drag it across your timeline, you'll be able to see what your animation will look like.

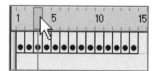

You can also see what it will look like if you test your Flash movie by selecting Control > Test Movie, but the animation is quite small, so you won't see the full details unless you choose View > Zoom In.

Tweening

We've just animated something by going through it frame by frame. It's taken us a while to do just fourteen frames, and our movie is running at 24 frames a second, so it could take us a long time to do things this way. Fortunately, there is a way to speed all this up. In classic animations, such as the Walt Disney ones that you'll have watched when you were younger, the top animators frequently drew the start and end frames of an animation and left a junior member of staff to draw the in between frames.

The good news here is that you don't have to wait around for years to get promoted before someone will draw your in between frames – Flash will do it for you right now. In Flash, this is called **tweening** (which comes, as you'll have worked out by now, from "in betweening"). Just as the old animators did, you need to have a start and an end point – two keyframes on your timeline.

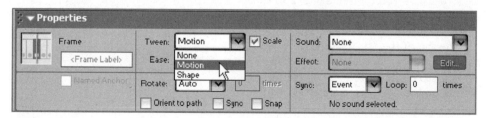

Tweens can only be used when the objects that you're tweening have been turned into symbols, in the same way that we turned our butterfly into a graphic symbol just now. Draw something on the stage, try and tween it, and it doesn't work? Always check that it's been made into a symbol before you throw Flash out of the window.

You'll notice that there are two types of tweens available to you when you select the Tween: drop-down menu in the Properties inspector: **Motion** and **Shape**. Motion tweens are used for adding movement to objects like our butterfly, whilst shape tweens are used to morph one shape into another. We're going to be looking at Motion tweens here, but we'll take a quick look at Shape Tweens before we finish.

> *Not only is tweening easier, but it leaves less information for Flash to store, making for smaller files and faster download/display times.*

1. We've looked at the timeline, but life would get pretty boring if we could only have one item on the stage at any one time. To solve this problem, Flash has **layers**. These work just like you think they might: like sheets of acetate lain on top of each other. Create a new layer now by clicking on the **Insert Layer** button, as shown (it's at the bottom left-hand corner of the timeline).

2. You should now have two layers, appropriately called Layer 1 and Layer 2. When you get more than a few layers, it's difficult to remember what you put on each one, so it's best to call your layers after what you put on them. Double-click on the Layer 1 text, and type in butterfly to replace it. Double-click on the Layer 2 text on the other layer, and replace that with the word string.

3. In Flash, if one layer obscures another, the layer at the top is always displayed as the top, or first layer, that the viewer sees. In the screenshot, you can see a line, a square, and a circle, and how they appear: the square on top of everything else, because it is at the top of the list of layers. Here, we want our string layer above butterfly, but you can easily move them by (single-) clicking on the layer name and dragging it

up and down in the list of layers.

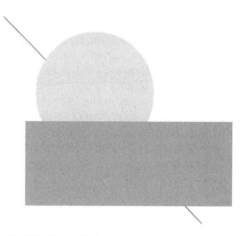

4. What we're going to do now is draw a line for our butterfly to fly along, and then tween our butterfly along that line. Right-click on your string layer to see the list of options for that layer, and choose Guide.

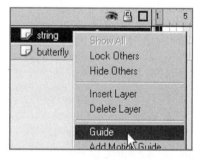

5. You'll now see a little hammer icon to the left of your string layer. It doesn't know which layer it is going to guide yet, so click on your butterfly layer, and drag it onto the string layer. When you've done this, the butterfly layer should indent, a different icon will appear to the left of string, and a dotted line will show up between the two layers (as shown in the screenshot).

6. Select the keyframe at the beginning of the string guide layer, and draw a path for the butterfly to follow with the **Pencil** tool. Don't make this too long – butterflies don't usually appear for long: they quickly flutter past and then disappear again. I've gone for a path from the middle to the top right, as shown in the screenshot.

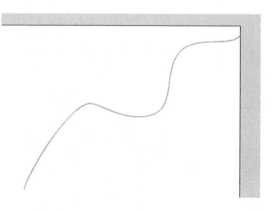

7. Now what we need to do is set the registration point of the butterfly to the end of the line. Select the butterfly, make sure **Snap to Objects** is turned on in the Tools panel (that's the Magnet symbol towards the bottom that we met in the last section). Drag the butterfly so it "snaps" to the end of the line. You'll notice that when it snaps there is a dark circle that shows you where it's snapping to.

8. Time to sort out our tween. Select frame 120 of the `butterfly` layer (at 24 frames per second, that's less than six seconds of time), and insert a keyframe. Insert a keyframe in the same place on the `string` layer.

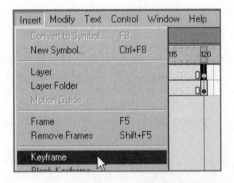

9. On the last frame of the `butterfly` layer, drag the butterfly up so that it's on the other end of the path you've created for it. Make sure it "snaps" to the line again.

10. Right-click on your `butterfly` layer, and select the `Create Motion Tween` option. The layer will now turn blue, and an arrow will represent the length of your tween. Drag the playhead through the frames to see how your butterfly now moves.

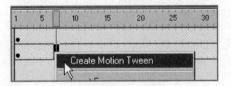

You could also have created a Motion Tween by clicking any frame between the first and last keyframes, and selecting `Motion Tween` *from the* `Tween:` *drop-down menu in the Property inspector.*

11. At the moment, our butterfly moves quite well, but always stays perfectly horizontal. Select any one of the frames in the tween, and check the `Orient to path` option in the Property inspector to rotate the butterfly appropriately as it flies along. Drag the playhead along the tween again to see the effect this has.

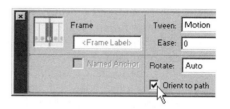

12. Butterflies don't always fly at the same speed, either. Sometimes, they hover over one spot. Find a place in your tween where you think you'd like the butterfly to pause a moment (I've chosen frame 80). Add two keyframes, one after the other. Select the first keyframe, and add some frames – you can use Insert > Add Frame each time, but F5 is a lot quicker. I've added ten frames, so that the pause lasts from frame 80 to frame 90, but experiment and see what seems right for your butterfly.

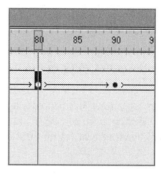

13. As a result of the extra frames you've just added to the `butterfly` layer, you'll need to go and extend the `string` layer so that they both end in the same place. Simply drag the end keyframe across to the new end frame.

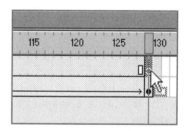

14. We can also alter the speed at which our butterfly tackles the path. Select the first frame of the layer. In the Property inspector, drag the Ease bar (found just underneath the `Tween:` menu, as shown) up to the maximum value of `100`.

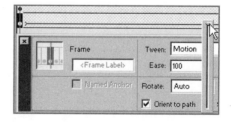

15. Now select another frame later on – I've selected frame 60, where my butterfly reaches the top of a curve, so might speed up a little – and set the `Ease:` value to the minimum value of `-100`. Test your movie with CTRL+ENTER, and watch the effect. Your butterfly should start off moving slowly, and start to move faster. My butterfly moves faster, then hovers, then disappears off the screen, so I'm quite happy with the effect and I'm going to leave it at that. You might want to add some more keyframes to create more pauses, or to adjust the butterfly manually with the Free Transform tool. You could also experiment with different easing routines to suit your path.

Shape Tweening

We mentioned shape tweening briefly earlier, and it works in pretty much the same way as Motion Tweening. We're not going to use much shape tweening in our site, but let's take a quick look.

1. Open up a new Flash movie, and call it `butterfly_shape_tween.fla`. Create a blank keyframe at frame 50.

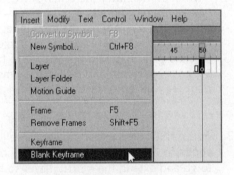

2. Use the Brush tool set to a fairly large circular size to add a brown splodge to the first keyframe.

3. In `butterfly_animation.fla`, select the butterfly graphic, and double-click so that you're editing it in place. Highlight the butterfly, and select Edit > Paste (don't forget

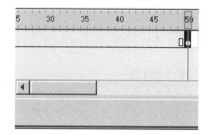

to double-click so that you select the fill **and** the stroke, or you'll end up with just the orange or just the black parts). Switch to `butterfly_shape_tween.fla`, select frame 50, and go to Edit > Paste.

> It's really important that you paste the butterfly as a collection of lines and fills, and not as a symbol. Confusingly, Flash needs graphics to be symbols to Motion Tween them, but **can't** Shape Tween symbols. If you see that blue bounding box appear around your butterfly on the stage to indicate that it's a graphic symbol, delete it and try again, or your shape tween won't work.

4. With a brown splodge on frame one, and a butterfly on frame 50, select a frame in between the two, and select `Shape Tween` from the `Tween:` drop-down menu in the Property inspector. You'll see an arrow to denote the tween as before, but the layer will turn to green rather than blue this time.

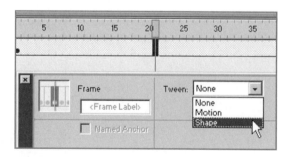

5. Run your playhead through the results (or press CTRL+ENTER) and you'll see a butterfly emerge from its coccoon.

Of course, if you get adventurous, then you could create a whole animation, starting by motion tweening a caterpillar moving along one of the leaves you created in the last chapter, then shape tweening it into a pupus and then a butterfly, and finally motion tweening the butterfly across the stage as a it lives out the last few beautiful moments of its life. Stunning animations like the goober story at http://www.goober.nu grow from such small initial ideas.

Further steps

Hopefully, this session has shown you some of the tremendous animation power that Flash offers. To practice what we've learned about animating along paths, try taking one of our leaves from the last chapter and animating it along a path — not forgetting some easing to add some of that real-life "fluttering" motion as it makes its way from the tree to the ground. Check out `leaf_paws_01` to see my version in action.

> *Remember, you can only tween one object on a single layer at once. If you've got more than one object on a layer, and you want to tween only one, try using* Modify > Distribute to Layers *to split up the objects.*

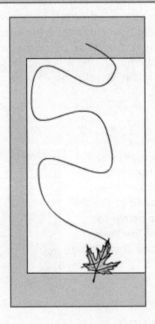

We'll be moving onto other topics in the following sessions, but don't think we've forgotten our butterfly and the leaf animation above, because we'll be coming back to add them to our site in a later session.

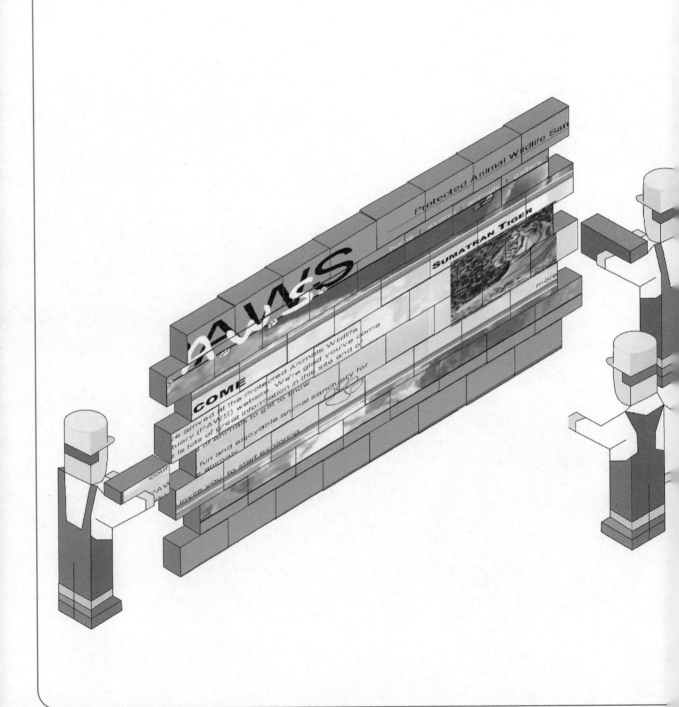

Using Imported Graphics

So far, we've looked at creating graphics in Flash. Using graphics created with other programs, or taken with digital cameras, can also be important in creating a visually impressive Flash site. Just take a look at www.siliconbauhaus.com or www.2advanced.com to see how graphics created elsewhere can add to a Flash site. In this session, we're going to use a photo to create a background for our main site.

The three most common formats you'll use for working with Flash are GIF, JPEG, and PNG. The problem with bringing in graphics in these formats is that that they add up to make a much greater file size than the images we've created in Flash. This means that we have to be careful about the size and number of images, and the way we use them in Flash.

Importing scanned images

To begin with, we're going to look at importing a scanned image. We've got a scrap of paper with a logo concept sketched on it, and have scanned the image. We'll import it into Flash so we can "trace" the footprint and use the image as a guide for adding text in the next session.

1. Create a new Flash movie, and save it as `logo.fla`. Select File > Import and choose the file called `logo.gif` from the CD. You'll see the sketch appear on the stage, with a dotted gray border signifying that the item is bitmap-based. (If you look in the Library, you'll see a little tree icon that signifies a bitmap image.)

2. Add a new layer and call it `Traced`. Name the original layer `Logo`, and lock it by clicking the second dot (under the padlock symbol), as shown in the screenshot. This will lock the layer, so that you won't be able to draw on the image layer. This means that we can delete the `logo` layer when finished so that we have a copy of our logo without the file size created by an imported graphic.

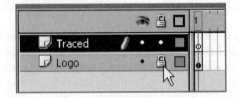

3. Select the Pencil tool, and set it to `Smooth`, choose a solid stroke thickness of 1 in the Property inspector, and choose a bright color (red, for example) so that you can clearly see your line when you draw over the sketch.

4. Work your way around all of the sections of the paw print on the left - don't worry about the text and the lines, we'll add them later. If you're not happy with the results you get drawing freehand with the Pencil, then try the Pen tool.

Remember that zooming in always helps when you're trying to draw accurately in Flash.

5. To see the results of your drawing clearly, hide the `logo` layer by clicking on the "dot" to the left of the padlock icon, underneath the eye symbol.

6. When you're happy with your lines (this is a natural footprint, so don't worry too much about minor irregularities), select them all, and use Insert > Convert to Symbol to convert your paw into a graphic symbol called `logo_outline`. We don't want to include any of the original sketch here, so keep the `logo` layer hidden. Check to make sure the Registration setting in the Convert to Symbol dialog has the black square in the middle, as shown.

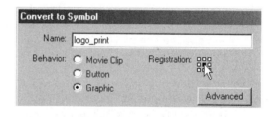

7. We've got our paw print sorted, so save your file, and we'll return to our logo in the next session to add some color and shading.

Working with imported photos

What if you want to alter a picture after you import it? One of the nice things about Flash MX is that it has what Macromedia call **round trip** graphic editing capabilities. This means that it can send an image out to an editing program, let you alter it, and then update your Flash movie with the altered file.

If you want to give this a try, right-click an imported image in the library (I've used `baby_duck_03` in the example), and you'll see a menu pop up. Select `Edit with Fireworks`, if you're lucky enough to have Fireworks, otherwise, select `Edit With` and specify your image editing application of choice. Edit your image, save, exit, and return to Flash, where you'll find that your graphic has been updated.

We've already prepared the two graphics we're going to use here, so we're not going to look at using applications like Paint Shop Pro, Fireworks, Photoshop Elements or even Photoshop itself, in any greater detail. If you're interested in learning more about using these programs to manipulate images, then friends of ED has a wide range of books on these subjects – check out www.friendsofed.com for further details.

1. Create a new Flash movie, and save it as `paws_01.fla`. Select Modify > Document and give it a size of 640x480 pixels and a frame rate of 24fps.

2. Use File > Import to import `red_001.jpg` from the CD. Flash will detect that there is also a `red_002.jpg` on the CD, and ask whether you want to import all the images in the sequence. Select `Yes`, and the two images will be copied into the first two frames of your Flash movie.

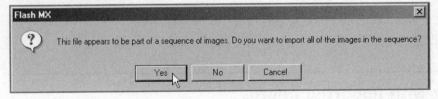

3. Select the image on the first frame, and convert it to a graphic symbol called `red_01`. Check that it's turned up in your library, and delete it from the stage. Repeat

this process with `red_02.jpg`. Your library should now have the two images, and the two graphic symbols in it.

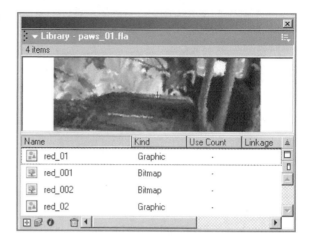

4. Delete the first frame by selecting it and going to Insert > Remove Frames. This should leave you with the `red_002` graphic symbol that you've just created. Select Window > Align and the Align window will appear, as shown. Select the `To Stage` button, which means that we're going to align our picture relative to the stage, and not relative to another item on the stage. Center your image vertically and horizontally by clicking on the `Align Vertical Center` and the `Align Horizontal Center` buttons, as indicated on the screenshot. You should be able to visually see your picture align to the center of the stage.

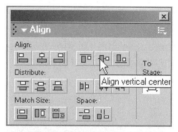

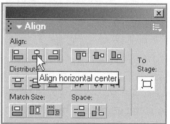

5. Rename the layer `red_02`, and create a new layer called `red_01`. Hide the red_02 layer by clicking on the black dot under the eye symbol, as we did in the last session.

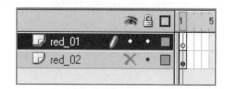

6. Drag the `red_01` graphic onto this new layer. Center it in the same way that we've just centered `red_01`. If you make `red_02` visible again, and switch between making `red_01` visible and invisible, you'll see that `red_01` is an enlargement of the center of the picture. We're going to add an effect to

this in the next step.

7.   Select the graphic on the `red_02` layer. In
the Property inspector, click on the `Color`
option on the right, and select `Tint` from
the drop-down menu. Make sure the color
chip is white, and use the slider bar to set
the tint to 30% (as shown). Repeat this for
the top layer, but set the tint to 80% instead.

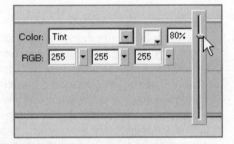

> *We could adjust the* `Alpha` *setting in the* `Color Mixer` *window for
> the same effect, but Alpha tends to affect the playback of files if we
> overuse it, so we used* `tint` *instead.*

8.   Your image should now look something like
the one pictured, with the lighter band
through the middle: this is where we will
place our site content in future sessions.

9. As we've said, imported pictures do tend to add a lot of file size to a Flash Movie. Flash is usually set to compress all images by 50% using JPG compression, and in this example it's doing a great job. The images we imported total around 42kb, but come down to 18kb when exported from Flash. We can further customize the quality and compression for each image. In the Library, right-click on `red_002` – that's the original image, listed as a bitmap, and not the graphic symbol. Select `Properties` from the menu. In the `Bitmap Properties` window, turn off the `Use document default quality` option.

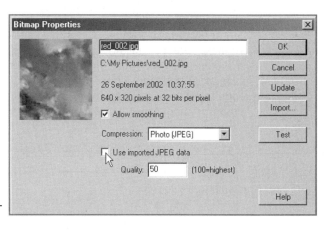

10. In the box that appears, play around with the `Quality:` setting, and use the `Test` button to see the results. I've gone with 35%, as it still gives a nice clean image.

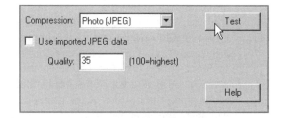

11. Repeat this for the other image. I've set this to 15%. Because the image is tinted white, it's very hard to see any of the distortion caused by the compression. Save your file, and then test it.

12. The last things to add are some horizontal lines, so create a new layer called `lines`. Select the Line tool from the Tools panel. In the Property inspector, set the color to black and the width to three pixels, using the slider bar.

13. Draw a horizontal line across the stage (hold
SHIFT down whilst dragging across the stage
to make sure it's straight). It doesn't matter
if the line is slightly wider than the stage, as
long as it's not short. Choose the Arrow
tool, select your line, and convert it to a
graphic symbol called `black_line_size_3`.

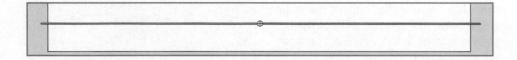

14. Move the line above the beginning of the
bottom graphic. With the line still selected ,
and then hold down the SHIFT key and select
the `red_02` image. Both the line and the
image should now be selected. Bring up the
Align panel again, and make sure that the
To Stage option is turned off. Select `Align
bottom edge` and your line should fit per-
fectly along the bottom of the graphic. This
will align both graphics to whichever is the
lower, which is why your line needs to be
above the bottom of the graphic when you
select this option.

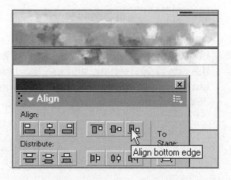

15. Select your `lines` layer, and drag another
line out of your Library and onto the stage.
Make sure that your line is below the top of
the `red_02` image. Select `red_02` and the
new line (using SHIFT as before), and bring
up the Align panel. This time, select `Align
top edge`.

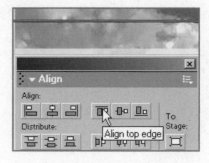

16. Working on the `lines` layer, drag two more
lines onto the stage, tint them 100% white,
and align them to the `red_01` image. These
lines provide a visual barrier, holding back
the white of our page. Don't worry if your
lines stick out a little at the edges: remember that that the person viewing your SWF
can only see what is on the stage area, and

anything that sticks out over the edge of
that will be invisible. Save your file.

Further steps

In this session, we've seen how to import images into Flash, and how to make sure that they don't inflate
our file size too much. We've done this in two ways. Firstly, we traced the original image, and deleted it
once we'd traced it. Secondly, we applied some effects and reduced the quality of the images to produce
an eye-catching background for our site.

You've probably got some images, or digital photos, or maybe even material to scan lying around, so we'll
leave it up to you to go away and have some fun with what we've learned here. We're going to create a
slide show of some of the PAWS pictures later on, so you'll be able to present any pictures you do find
in a nice Flash interface before the end of the book.

You might also want to experiment with the Trace Bitmap function, found in the Modify menu. This makes
Flash automatically trace an image in the same way as we did manually at the beginning of the session.
Be careful here: setting the detail high can create file sizes even bigger than the original, as Flash will try
to trace every little line in the photo.

We haven't used Trace Bitmap in the PAWS site, because it loses too much accuracy in the images of animals we're using. With a different type of picture (such as those shown) and with some low detail settings, it can help make some really creative images.

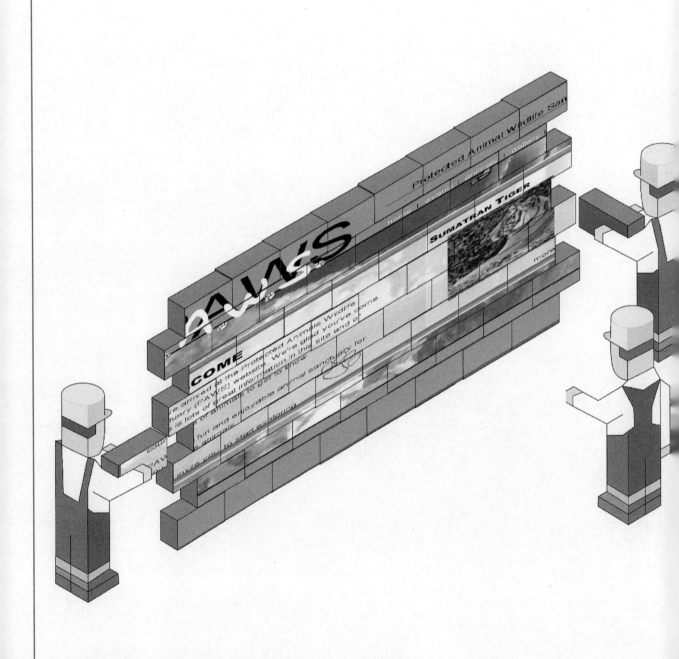

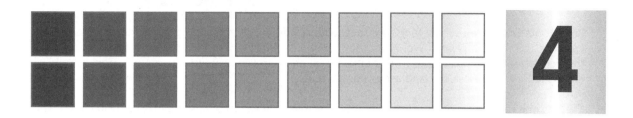

Text and Fills

In this session, we'll explore the use of text in Flash. As you'll see, if you select the Text tool and look in the Property inspector, there are three types of text in Flash: **static**, **dynamic**, and **input**. We're going to be concentrating on static text in this session – in other words, text that we enter that cannot be changed by the user.

> *Dynamic text and Input text are used in conjunction with ActionScript. Dynamic text is text that can be altered (an updated list of news headlines, for example), and input text is text entered by a user (in a form, for example). We'll be using dynamic text to load our events page in from a* .TXT *file later on.*

Before we dive in to take a look, we've got the issue of **fonts** to consider. Some fonts look different in Flash. In the screenshot, the top text is arial and the bottom text is in _sans.

This is a block of text that will wrap
itself when the line I'm typing gets too
long for one or two lines.

This is a block of text that will wrap
itself when the line I'm typing gets too
long for one or two lines.

When we use a font like the arial in the screenshot, Flash embeds a copy of the font in our SWF – making the SWF bigger, and slower to load as the fonts will be loaded in before any other content. It also **anti-aliases**, or smoothes the outline of the font, which is why the arial looks a bit blurry in the shot above.

_sans, on the other hand, is a **device font** – which means that Flash will look on the user's machine for the default sans font and use that. The plus point is that Flash won't anti-alias device fonts and make them look blurry when you're using small sizes. The minus point is that it takes control away from you: if the user doesn't have the same font you've used, then your design is going to look fairly different.

Pixel fonts (also called screen fonts) are fonts built around pixels and are used only for display on screen. (You *can* use them to print in Word, but they'll look a bit blocky.) The `fff pacific` font you can see in the screenshot is a pixel font from Fonts for Flash (http://www.fontsforflash.com). These fonts are embedded into the Flash file, and act as normal fonts.

There is one catch: pixel fonts **must** be placed at whole pixel values on a stage that has whole pixel width and height values to look good. In the screenshot, the top line of text is sitting at (103, 128) on the stage, and looks fine. The bottom line of text is sitting at (103.5, 133.3), which causes it to blur.

This text is FFF Pacific 8
This text is FFF Pacific 8

1. Open up `logo.fla` from the last session. Delete the `logo` layer by right-clicking on it and selecting `Delete Layer`. You should now be left with the `traced` layer, with the paw print on it.

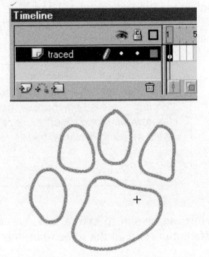

2. Select the paw print, and use the Property inspector to give it a width of 250 pixels and a height of 205 pixels.

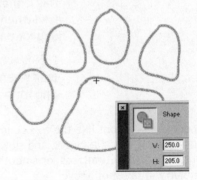

3. With the outline still selected, use the Property inspector to turn it black, and specify a `Hairline` stroke size

4. We're going to be doing some work with our logo, so we're going to create a container graphic symbol, to contain all the separate bits that we work on in one. Create a graphic symbol, and call it `logo_complete`.

5. Double click the new symbol to edit it, and rename the default layer `impressions`

6. Select your newly pasted `logo_outline`, and choose Modify > Break Apart. The Break Apart command reduces our graphic symbol into a set of ungrouped editable elements, so that we can add some colors to the paw.

7. Select the Paint Bucket tool from the Tools panel, and select a fill color of #666666 (a dark gray) — either enter the code directly into the box, or choose the gray from the top left-hand side.

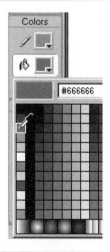

8. Fill each of the paw areas. Delete the outside lines, so that just the fills remain. You should have something like the screen shot.

9. Select the solid area by clicking on the first, the SHIFT - clicking on the rest, and convert it to a graphic symbol called logo_solid. As before, make sure that the registration point is in the middle.

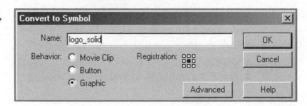

10. Footprints are very seldom as solid as our print, so let's soften it a little. You should still be in logo_complete – check this by looking at the text next to the Scene 1 text Select the logo_solid graphic symbol that you've just created, and select Modify > Break Apart.

> *You may be wondering why we're bothering to make our paw prints into graphic symbols if we're just going to break them apart into strokes and fills again. The answer is that when we create symbols, Flash keeps a copy of the graphic for us that we can come back to, and we'll be doing just that in later sessions.*

11. We want to create the effect shown - paws are soft and create deep impressions near the center that soften out near the edges. We can use **gradients** to achieve this effect.

12. Highlight the left toe impression, and select Window > Color Mixer. Select Radial from the drop down list. You will see your pad take on a black to white gradient from center to edge.

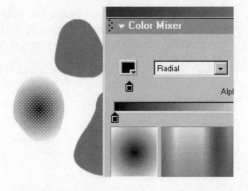

13. Click on the gray color marker on the left of the gradient – it looks like a house, with a little roof, which will change to black when you click on it. Change the color to `#9F9F9F` (a pale gray).

14. Now select the white "house" at the other end of the scale, and make sure it's set to `#FFFFFF` (white). Using the slider at the right of the gradient scale, set the gray house color's alpha setting to `28%`. Set the white house color's alpha setting to `0%`.

If you accidentally click at a different point on the gradient, you may well create another "house" symbol on the line, whose color and alpha values you can also alter. This can be useful in creating more complex gradients. For the moment, click and drag down to remove it.

15. This looks good, but the fill is very circular. Select the **Fill Transform tool** from the Tools panel (it's just above the Paint Bucket Tool). Click on the fill, and you'll see a circle with a square and 2 circles on it. These are the control handles: the square allows you to pull/push the circle into an ellipse, the first circle controls scale and the last controls rotation. Push the circle of gradient into an ellipse, and make it a bit bigger.

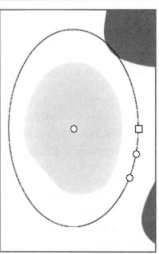

16. Now click on the control handle in the middle, and use this to lift the fill higher.

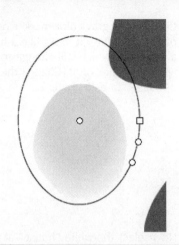

17. Your gradient will stay set until you choose something else, so you can now use the Paint Bucket tool to fill the other paws, and the Fill Transform tool to adjust these. Your initial mouse click with the Paint Bucket tool will be the center around which the radial gradient will circle. The approach that you'll have to take with the Fill Transform tool won't always be the same – I had to make the oval a bit larger with several of the other toes.

18. Select all of your paw print gradients (not the strokes), and convert them to a graphic symbol called `logo_pad_impressions`.

19. Add a second Layer inside `logo_complete`. Open the Library, and drag a copy of `logo_solid` into it. Position this at (125, 102.5) so that it covers the gradients exactly.

20. Select the instance of `logo_solid`, and choose `Tint:` from the Color: drop-down menu in the Property inspector. Choose white from the Color menu immediately to the right of this, and `100%` from the menu immediately to the right of this. Drag the layer with the now invisible `logo_solid` on underneath the layer with `logo_pad_impressions`, and our original gradients should become visible again.

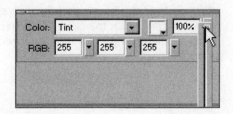

Adding the text

If you remember the original sketch, it had some text next to the logo, so we'll add that before we finish.

1. Select all of `logo_complete` on the stage by drawing a box around it so that both the gradient fills and surrounding lines are highlighted. convert this to a graphic symbol called `logo_and_text` Go to Window > Transform, and enter a value of −14.5 into the Rotate field.

2. In `logo_and_text`, call the default layer `print`, and add a new layer called `text`.

3. Select all of the logo on the print layer (make sure both the gradient fill and the outline are selected), and re-size and re-position it to the values shown in the screenshot.

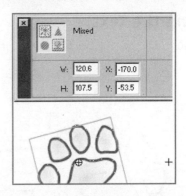

4. Select the Text tool from the Tools panel, and look at the Property inspector. You should see many of the standard features for editing text: the normal bold and italic buttons, the alignment buttons for left, center, right and justify, a drop down with fonts and a font size slider. Select arial black, a size of 70, and character spacing of -10 to create some slight overlapping for effect. (The color should be black by default.)

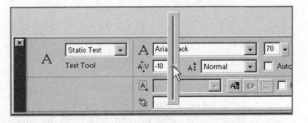

5. Click on the stage to the right of the logo. You should see a box appear. Type the word PAWS in capitals. Select the Arrow tool again, select the text, and set its X and Y positions to -59 and -54 in the Property inspector.

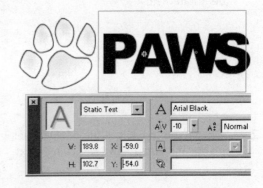

6. The last thing to add to this is the tag line that we'll put above the text we've just added. Select the Text tool, and choose _sans size 11. (_sans is a device font, and Flash will rely on the user's machine to supply the font, meaning that it won't anti-alias it, and cause it to become blurred and unreadable at the smallish size of 11.) Change the spacing back to 0. Type in protected animal wildlife sanctuary in lower case.

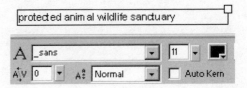

7. To line it up above the PAWS text, set its X and Y settings to -54 and -40. This should position the text just above the text, as shown.

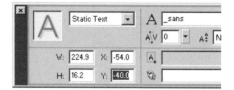

8. Save your file. Select logo_and_text, and go to Edit > Copy. Open up PAWS_01.fla from the last session, and add a new layer called logo to the main timeline. Drag this layer to the top of the other layers, select the first keyframe in it, and select Edit > Paste. In the Property inspector, set the X and Y positions to 0,0, and the logo should line up nicely at the top of our screen.

Further Steps

Congratulations - you've reached the first significant milestone in Flash knowledge: you're now in full command of the interface, the drawing tools, and the ways in which you can add pictures and text to a Flash movie.

We've done a lot in this session, so you may just want to take well-deserved rest! If not, then there's plenty of opportunity for using what we've learned about gradients to add some slightly more convincing autumnal hues to those leaves we created earlier. Either that, or have a go at your own logo.

After this session, you probably never want to see another graphic symbol again, so it's just as well we're going to be taking a look at the graphic symbol's bigger and more powerful brother - the movie clip – in the next session.

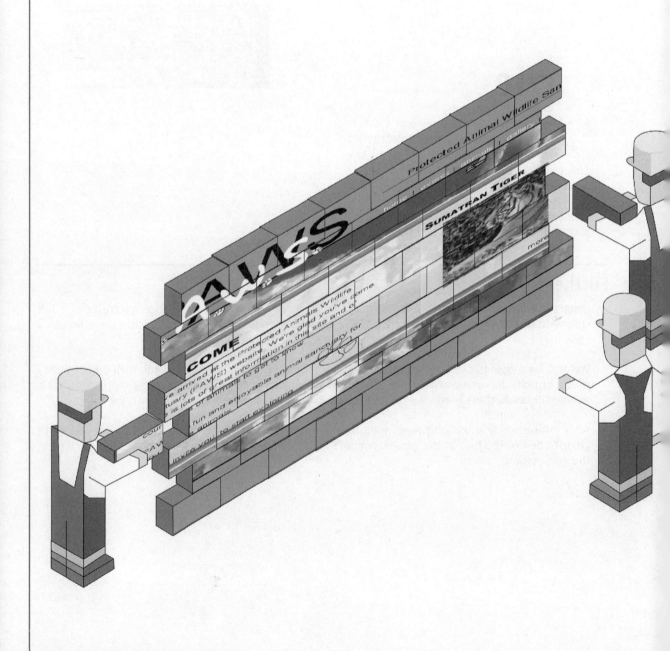

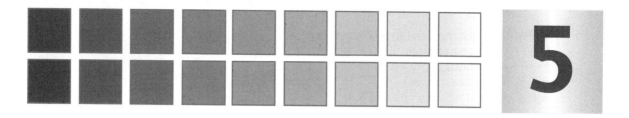

Complex Animations with Movie Clips

In this session, we're going to move on from graphic symbols and take a look at the more versatile **movie clip** symbol.

Movie symbols have their own timeline that can operate separately from the main timeline. This means that while the main timeline can be stopped, our movie clips can continue to play. They still play at the same frame rate as the main timeline, but operate separately. Movie clips can contain anything the main timeline contains - images, scripts, audio, and so on. They can even contain other movie clips, a process which is called **nesting**.

Why use a movie clip instead of the main timeline? Timelines can get very crowded very quickly, and movie clips allow us to organize things a little better. We might also want to use these animations in another Flash movie. With movie clips, we can store these animations as symbols, and we can then drag them out of our library into another Flash movie (we'll be doing this later with some of our animations).

There's another reason: if you remember back to Session 2, we animated a butterfly graphic symbol. In the graphic symbol, we animated the butterfly so that its wings were moving. Back on the main timeline, we animated the butterfly so that it moved along a particular path. In other words, we coupled two effects (wings flapping and moving) together to make a much more sophisticated animation. With movie clips, we can do even more of this.

1. You may remember that, at the end of Session 2, we suggested that you animate one of the leaves from Session 1 falling from top to bottom. If you've done this, great – go and open it up now. If not, open up `leaf_paws_01.fla` from the CD.

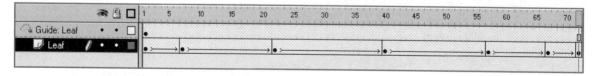

2. Highlight the Leaf layer and its guide layer either by clicking and dragging down and across from the first keyframe, or by SHIFT-clicking on the layers. Select Edit > Copy Frames (the normal Copy option will be grayed out, so make sure you scan all the way down to the Copy Frames option) to make a copy of the frames and all the items required by those frames.

3. Create a new Flash movie, and call it `ran-dom_effects.fla`. Use Modify > Document to give it our usual size of 640 x 480 and an fps setting of 24. Inside this, select Insert > New Symbol, choose Movie Clip, and name the new symbol `rndm_leaf_01`. Click OK.

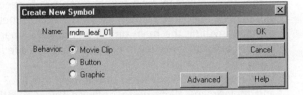

4. Select the first frame of your movie clip, and use Edit > Paste Frames to paste the frames into the timeline. Your two layers will be added.

5. Just as when you're editing a graphic symbol, you'll see that the name of your new symbol appears to the right of the Scene 1 text in the top left hand corner (just underneath your timeline). Return to the main timeline by clicking on the Scene 1 text, and rename Layer 1 `Leaf`.

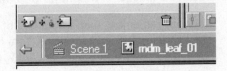

> *It's really important to keep an eye on this text and check whether you're on the main timeline or inside a movie clip. It's very easy to make a mistake and edit the wrong thing!*

6. Whenever you create a symbol, or import a file to use, Flash will store it away for you in the **library**. Go and open this now, with Window > Library, and you'll see the two items in your Flash movie: the `leaf_01` graphic symbol, and the `rndm_leaf_01` movie clip that we've just created.

7. Select the `rndm_leaf_01` movie clip, and drag it out onto the main stage so that it's sitting just above the top left corner. Use your cursor keys to fine tune the leaf's position so that it's positioned as shown. Placing it off stage means someone viewing the Flash movie won't be able to see the leaf when they first look at this movie, but if you press CTRL+ENTER to test your movie, you'll see the leaf fall from the top of the screen to the bottom guided by the information in the movie clip.

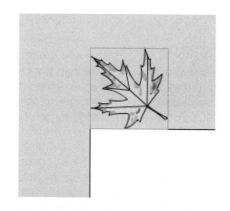

8. With your movie clip selected on the stage, select Insert > Convert to Symbol, and make a new movie clip called `leaf_collection`. Set the Registration point to the top left by clicking on the square in the top-left to move the highlight.

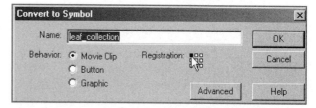

> When naming your movie clips, remember that they must start with a letter (a to z) and must not start with a number or symbol (_ # *). While you can use spaces in your names, it's common practice to replace the space with an _ underscore - `myMovie_clip`, for example.

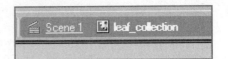

9. We're going to start to "nest" our movie clips by placing one movie clip in another. Double-click on the movie clip on the stage to edit `leaf_collection` – you should see `leaf_collection` come up next to Scene 1 at the top-left of your screen.

10. Rename the first layer `leaf_01` and create a new layer called `leaf_02`. On `leaf_02`, create a blank keyframe in frame 6 and add a copy of `rndm_leaf_01` into it by dragging it out of the library and onto the keyframe on frame 6. Place it slightly further over than the other leaf (mine has an X position of about 170).

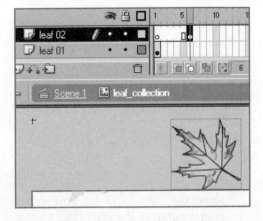

11. Drag your playhead through the first six frames, and you'll see a flashing effect because the movie clip tries to play and loops between displaying frames 1 and 6 continually. If you test the movie with CTRL + ENTER, then you won't see anything – the leaf movie clips never have enough time to fall before Flash moves on. What we need is to do is add enough frames to allow the animations in the movie clips to play through before the playhead returns to frame 1 and starts all over again.

12. Insert a blank keyframe using Insert > Blank Keyframe at frame 73 in the `leaf_01` layer (why 72? Remember we wanted our animation to last for three seconds, and 3 x 24fps is 72 – this was the length of our animations in the last session), and at frame 78 in the `leaf_02` layer. This allows each leaf time to float down and across. Test your movie now by pressing CTRL + ENTER, and you should have two leaves falling - one just after the other.

13. Add two more layers, call them `leaf_03` and `leaf_04`, and order the layers so that `leaf_04` is at the top and `leaf_01` is at the bottom. Add blank keyframes in frames 12 and 16, and in 82 and 86. Drag instances of `rndm_leaf_01` into the keyframes in frames 12 and 16, positioning them in between the leaves you've already placed.

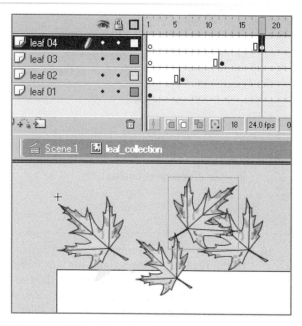

14. Test your movie, and return to the main timeline by clicking on Scene 1. We're going to play this animation over the top of our home page, so we need our leaves to look like they're on top of everything else. To help this, we're going to add a shadow to our leaf. Open your library, and double-click on `leaf_01` to edit it. Because we used `leaf_01` in all of our movie clips, any changes we make here will apply to all our movie clips.

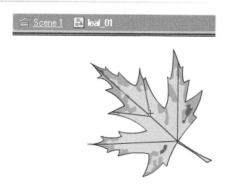

15. In `leaf_01`, rename the default layer `leaf`, and add a new layer called `shadow`. Drag the `shadow` layer so that it's underneath the `leaf` layer. Select the leaf in the `leaf` layer, and choose Edit > Copy. Select the `shadow` layer, and choose Edit > Paste in Place. Lock and hide the `leaf` layer so that we can't alter it.

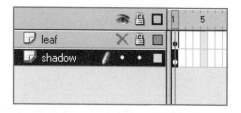

16. Select the leaf in our `shadow` layer, and convert it to a graphic symbol called `leaf_shadow`. With `leaf_shadow` still selected, press the right cursor key eight times, and then press the down cursor key eight times. This should move it just far enough away to make a good shadow, as you'll see if you make the `leaf` layer visible again for a moment as I have in the screenshot.

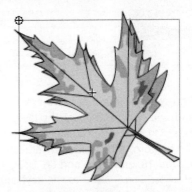

17. With `leaf_shadow` selected, choose Advanced from the drop-down Color menu in your Property inspector.

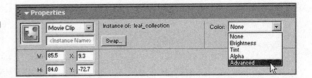

18. Click on the Settings button that will appear to the right of the menu, and the Advanced Effect box will appear. To make the shadow semi-transparent, give it xR, xG, and xB values of +153, and a xA value of −149. Click OK, and unlock the `leaf` layer and make it visible again.

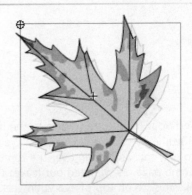

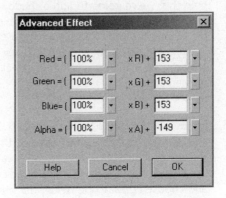

19. There's one last touch to add: go back to `leaf_collection`. Select the Free

Transform tool from the Tools panel, and rotate and res-size the four leaves to make them look a little more natural (you can also use `Modify > Transform > Flip Horizontal` to flip the leaves).

20. Save your file and test it. We now have a natural group of leaves falling, each with a shadow. Even better, we've done this with just four symbols, arranged as shown. That means that Joe Bloggs at home watching our site on his old computer only has to wait for four small symbols to download before this animation plays. Just think how many leaves we'd have if we hadn't got movie clips and graphic symbols!

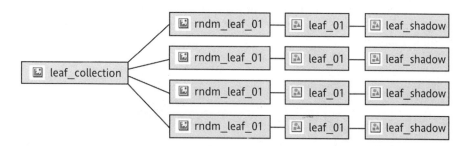

Further steps

We've already built a butterfly animation in Session 2, so try bringing this into `random_effects` as well. The steps are pretty much the same:

- Open up `butterfly_animation.fla`, and copy the frames we need from the main stage (don't forget to use Edit > Copy Frames, and not Edit > Copy).
- Create a new movie clip in `random_effects.fla`, and paste the frames into that.
- Return to the main timeline, and drag your movie clip onto the stage. In the final source file for this chapter, you'll see that I've used the Transform window to scale the butterfly to 150% of its original size, and have used the Info window to position it at (-31, 475).
- For extra effect, add a shadow layer to the `butterfly` graphic symbol. This will be a slightly longer task than the leaf, as you'll have to copy all 14 keyframes into the shadow layer, and then individually apply the Advanced Color Effect to each frame.
- Add some more butterflies if you want, as we did with the leaves. Make sure that you don't make things too busy, though – this animation will appear above other content in the final site.

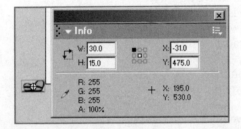

Test your movie when you're done, and you should see some animated leaves and butterflies. Later on (Session 14 to be exact), we'll add a small bit of script, so that these animations play randomly while people browse through the PAWS site. Speaking of the PAWS site, it's about time we got back to that, and we'll be adding some sound to it in the next session.

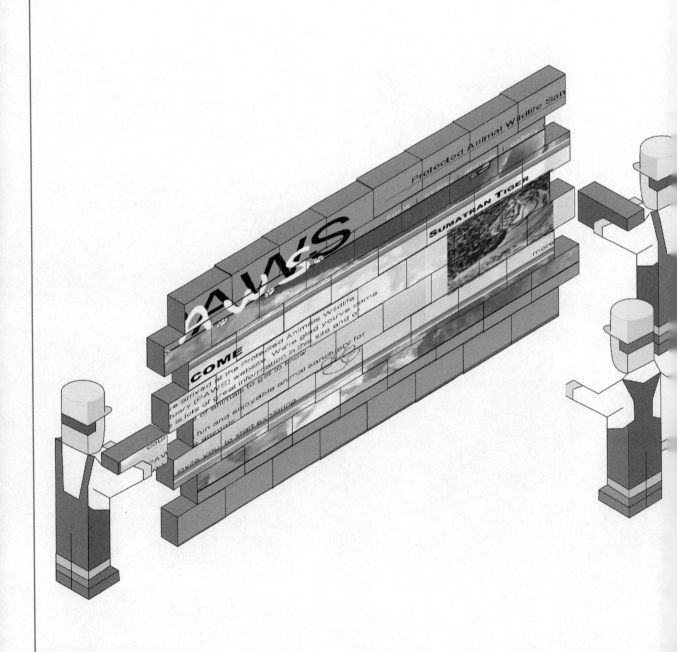

Adding Sound

Part of what sets Flash apart from the alternatives is the ease with which you can add multimedia elements, like sound and video, to your sites. In this session, we're going to add some sound to ours.

We want to give users an idea of the outdoor environment when they visit the PAWS site. One continuously looping track of bashing techno might suit a shopping site, but we need something more organic, so we'll aim for some natural and random sounds.

Our first step is to find out where we can obtain our sounds. One answer is to make them from scratch using applications like Fruity Loops, before using something like Sound Forge to optimize them. Just like graphics, sound needs filtering and optimizing to improve quality and decrease file size before it's used on the web.

While this may be an option you wish to investigate in the future, the reality is that, for the moment, we need to find some sounds prepared by someone else for us. There are quite a few sites on the web that exist just to offer you this. Among the best are:

http://www.meanrabbit.com
http://www.flashkit.com
http://www.findsounds.com
http://www.flashsound.com
http://www.sounds-for-flash.com/sounds.htm

The files that we're going to use in this session can be downloaded page 3 of the 'Nuclear Wav Storage Facility' at www.meanrabbit.com. For the first exercise you'll need peaceful.wav from the outdoor1.zip file, and for the second excercise, you'll need bird1.wav, bird2.wav, bird3.wav, and birdsong.wav from alotabird.zip

1. Create a new Flash movie, and save it as `audio.fla`. Give it the usual settings of 640 x 480, and 24 fps, and rename the first layer `audio`.

2. Use File > Import to import `peaceful.wav` into Flash. You'll notice that with audio, Flash puts assets directly into the Library.

3. Select the first frame and look in the Property inspector for the `sound` drop-down. This will give you a list of all the tracks in the Library. Choose the file you've just imported – `peaceful`. Save your Flash movie, and test it with CTRL+ENTER. You'll hear the audio track play once and then stop.

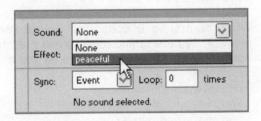

4. We want to loop this track – that is, play it over again when it reaches the end. When you played the track, you probably noticed that the volume increases at the start of the loop, so we need to rectify this as well. We could do this using software like Sound Forge, but Flash actually has a few tools that we can use here. In the Property inspector, hit the Edit button to open a window that allows us to edit the audio track.

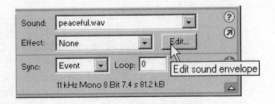

5. You'll see a large window open. The top track is the **left** channel and the bottom is the **right** channel. Both tracks have a line in them, with a white square at either end.

This is the audio line – otherwise known as the **envelope**. You can add more of these handles by clicking on the line, and you can then drag them up and down to increase or decrease the volume at different points in the sound file. The screenshot shown would pan the audio from left to right – the left track (at the top) goes from full volume to no volume, whilst the right track (at the bottom) goes from no volume to full volume.

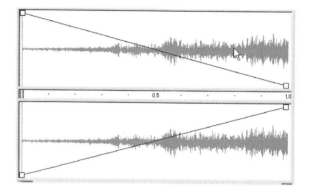

If you're thinking that the right and left channels look suspiciously similar, you're right. If you look at the Property inspector screenshot from the last step (or if you select the sound in the library), then you'll see that this is a mono sound file. Flash treats this as if it has two identical channels, rather than the two different channels you'd get with a stereo file.

6. Hit the zoom out button at the bottom of the window so we can see a little more of the wave pattern (as you'll probably discover, this is somewhat counter-intuitive as zooming **out**, with the minus sign, allows us to see more). You should see that the wave pattern itself – that's the wavy bit in the middle that looks a bit like a heart readout in a TV hospital drama – starts small and gets larger (or louder). The original author obviously wanted the track to fade in, while we just want it to start it at full volume

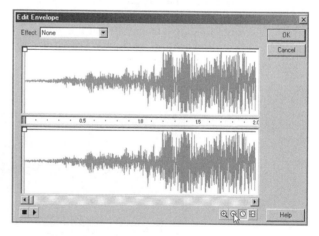

7. To solve this problem, we could try and increase the volume of the first part of the sound by dragging those handles up, so that the sound the user hears remains constant. This is going to be impossible to get absolutely right, though, so we're simply going to remove the first quiet bit from the equation.

We're going to adjust our **in**, or starting point. In between the left and right channels, there's a little timeline. Click on the handle at the far left of this, and drag it toward the larger part of the wave pattern (as shown). The background to the left of this will turn gray. Hit the play button in the bottom left-hand corner, and make sure that there's no fade at the beginning of the sound – if there is, drag the in handle a little further over and try again.

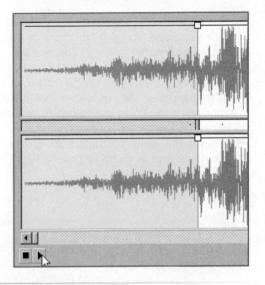

8. The line running along the top of the two tracks signifies that the audio is at full volume, which could detract from the calming effect we're aiming for and annoy our visitors. In the left track (at the top), click on the control handle and drag it down and to the left (you can't go past the first handle) until the line is about 20% of the way up from the bottom, as shown. Repeat this for the right track (at the bottom). Click OK when you've done this; we've finished editing our sound for the moment.

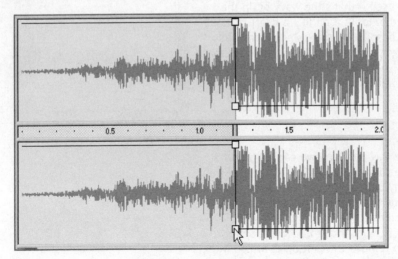

9. We have our audio, now we need to tell it to loop. We do this by telling Flash how many times we want it to loop in the Property inspector (if you can't see a box like the screenshot, expand your Property inspector by clicking on the arrow in the bottom right-hand corner). We want the loop to go on for as long as anyone is viewing the site – there isn't an infinity setting, but 99999 times is pretty much the same!

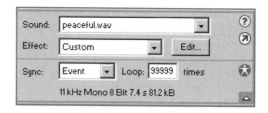

10. Save and test your Flash movie.

That's our sound file finished, but there's one more setting that we should mention before moving on. Next to the Loop box in the Property inspector, you should see a drop-down menu entitled Sync. This setting tells Flash how to load the sound:

- **Event** loads the sound in once in entirety, and we can use it as many times as we want to after that without having to load it in again.

- **Stream** sets the sound to stream in to play just once, and is tied to the timeline. This means the playhead will drop frames of animation from your movie in order to keep loading in the audio if it has to. It also means that frames must exist on the timeline for your audio to play.

If you're animating a talking character, you want the audio and animation to keep together. Using Stream can allow this to happen, as the audio becomes the master timekeeper. If the animation starts to get behind, Flash removes a frame of animation and checks to see if it has caught up with the audio. Obviously, we're looping our sound; so we want Event, which should be the default setting.

More sounds

We said at the beginning that we wanted some random sounds. Nature is not on a loop, and we need to reflect that. We have a very good reason for using a loop, though, Peaceful.wav was 80k to start with, and it's 12k when we export our SWF. If I created a ten-minute audio track from nature sounds, we'd have a huge file on our hands that would take up several megabytes at a minimum, and make our users wait for an age for the site to download.

What we're going to do to solve this is create a new file and randomly play a birdcall over the track we've just made, creating the illusion of a non-looping longer track whilst keeping our file size nice and low. We'll add a little bit of script to add the random bit in a little later on, but we can prepare the file here.

1. Create a new Flash movie, and save it as
    birdCalls_random.fla. Give it the usual
    settings: 640 x 480, 24 fps, and rename the
    first layer audio.

2. Import bird1.wav, bird2.wav,
    bird3.wav, and birdsong.wav into your
    Flash movie

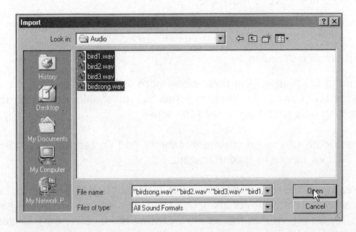

3. Create a new movie clip, and call it
    birdCall_01. Select the first frame, and
    choose bird1.wav from the Sound drop-
    down in the Property inspector.

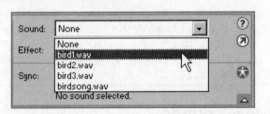

4. Open the envelope editor for this track by
    clicking on the Edit button. The timeline in
    the middle can either show time or frames,
    and you can select which you want by click-
    ing on the buttons at the bottom right-hand
    corner, next to the zoom buttons. Click on
    the frame view button, and you should see
    that this track lasts for just over 25 frames.

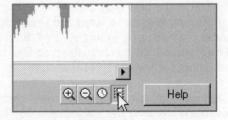

*If your wave pattern has a different length, check that your document is set to 24
fps. You can check this just below your timeline on the main stage, and double-click
this to bring up the Document Properties dialog to change it.*

5. The last thing we want is a loud birdcall
suddenly playing – that sort of thing leads
to scaring our visitors. Reduce the volume
to about one third of the maximum level, as
shown, and hit OK to return to the movie
clip.

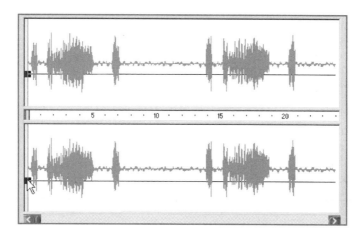

6. Rename the layer bc_01. In frame 30, insert
a blank frame (Insert > Frame). Your timeline should now show the blue wave pattern, which shows that your sound is present on that layer. As we worked out earlier,
the sound lasts a little longer than 25
frames, so we've allowed enough time for
the sound to finish playing. This stops the
audio track looping on top of itself – which
happens if the music is still playing when
the playhead has run out of frames and has
returned to frame 1.

7. Return to the main timeline. Add a
keyframe (Insert > Keyframe) in the second
frame of the audio layer. Select this, and
drag a copy of the birdCall_01 movie clip
you've just made onto the stage from the
library. You'll see that the movie clip doesn't
actually contain anything visible in it, so just
appears as a small crosshair. Place this in the
top left-hand corner of your movie, so you
know where to find it if you need it later.

8. We have one random birdcall ready to be called by some ActionScript. Now create three new movie clips called `birdCall_02`, `birdCall_03`, and `birdCall_04`. Follow steps 3 – 6 to add the audio for each. (`birdcall_02` and `birdcall_04` will need around 30 frames on their timelines, whilst `birdcall_03` is very short and will only need 15 frames.) Make sure you reduce the audio volume for each, otherwise all our previous care here will be undone when we blast a visitor with a loud sound file.

9. Return to the main timeline, and add three more blank keyframes to the `audio` layer. Drag the three movie clips onto these three keyframes, and save your file.

Further Steps

Later on, we'll not only make our audio play randomly, but we'll add a button to turn our audio on or off so that users have a choice about whether they want to listen or not. For now, though, we've done all the hard work of preparing our sound. The next session is also going to feature a bit of organization so that everything in our main site is ready for the content we'll be developing after that.

In terms of what else you can do with what you've learned in this session, the sky is your limit. Sound is one of the easiest ways to add atmosphere to a site, but it has to be chosen and used very carefully. Go and take a listen to some of the sounds available from the sites we mentioned earlier, or try just take a look at your hard disk and see what's there.

> *Flash will import MP3s as well as WAVs, so it's easy to transfer sound files from CD and into Flash by converting the sound into MP3 format with music players like the musicmatch jukebox (available from* www.musicmatch.com*). Files that you place on the web are subject to the same copyright restrictions as elsewhere, though - so don't use anything that you've not got permission to...*

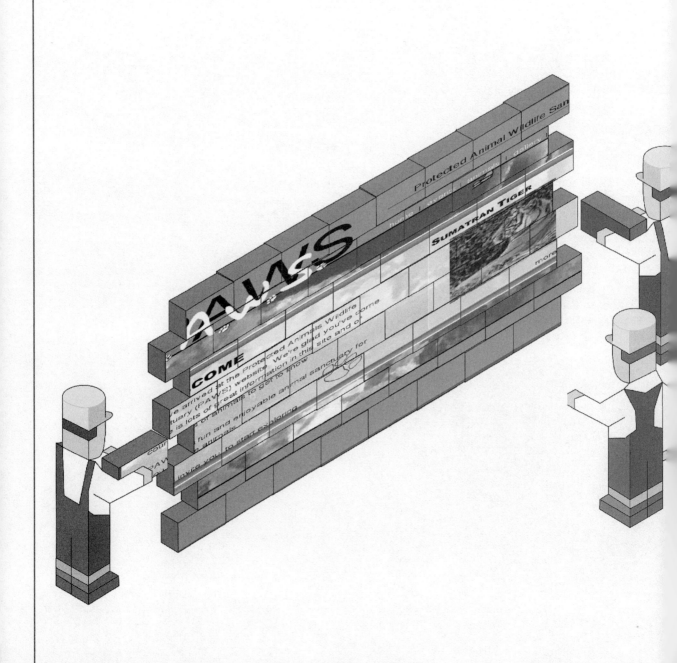

Layers and Labels

Well, we're only at Session 7, but we've already done a lot. You might not realize it, but you're already at the level that you'd have reached by the end of some other books, so well done. We've created quite a few graphic symbols and movie clips, and we've also imported some pictures and sounds. In the next session, we'll be covering the last of the three types of symbol: buttons.

First, though, things are getting a bit messy with all these assets lying around, so we're going to do some tidying. We're also going to set things up for our buttons, by inserting some **labels**. At the moment, you've only ever seen Flash play straight through a timeline by starting at the beginning and playing until the end.

What's nice, though, is that we can set Flash up so that it plays a timeline in a non-linear fashion. Let's imagine that we have three animations on our timeline: animation a on frame 1, animation b on frame 10, and animation c on frame 20. If Flash plays straight through this, then it'll play animation a, b, and then c. Labels allow us to identify a place where we can tell Flash to go to, so if we put labels on frames 1, 10, and 20, we could tell Flash to play animC, animA, and then animB.

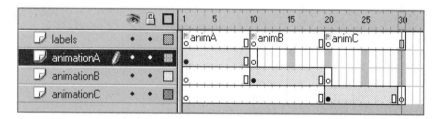

Some Flash users ignore labels because you can use frame numbers instead. So in our example, we could tell Flash to go to frame 10 when we wanted to play animB. This works fine, but the chances are that we will then decide to add an extra little bit to make animA a little bit more interesting, adding a few extra frames to make a better effect. When we now tell Flash to go to frame 10, it'll start playing halfway through our new animA. Arrrggghh!

With a label, Flash will always go to the label, wherever that label is. In other words, using frame numbers to tell Flash where to go means that once you do that, you can't alter the timeline without messing up everything else. With labels, it doesn't matter – you can mess around with that timeline as much as you want. It's also easier to remember what telling Flash to go to animC does than it is to remember what telling Flash to go to frame 302 does.

1. **Folders** are great for storing and organizing things, especially in the library. Open `birdCalls_random.fla` from the last session. Open up the library, and take a look in the bottom left-hand corner, you should see three icons: a blue cross, a folder, and a little `i` in a blue circle (the last icon is grayed out if a symbol in the library has not been highlighted).

2. These allow you to create new symbols (just as you would with Insert > New Symbol), create folders in the Library, and view the properties for the selected symbol, respectively. You can probably guess what we want to do here: click once on the New Folder icon, and a folder will appear in the Library window, waiting for a name. Call it `audio`.

3. Now click and drag the `bird1` sound onto the `audio` folder. Repeat this for the rest of the sound files. Double-click the folder to open it, and you'll see all your sound files neatly in one place. Double-click again and the folder will close, giving you a smaller main library, and a chance of finding what you're looking for in there. Save the Flash file and close it.

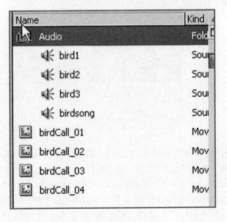

4. Open your main paws movie, (saved as `paws_01.fla` on the CD). The library here also needs some attention. Create three folders: `artwork`, `logo_bits`, and `photos`.

   ■ Place `black_line_size_3`, `red_01`, and `red_02` in `artwork`.

● Place `Logo_and_text`, `Logo_complete`, `Logo_outline`, `Logo_pad_impressions`, and `Logo_solid` in `logo_bits`.

● Place `red_001` and `red_002` in `photos`.

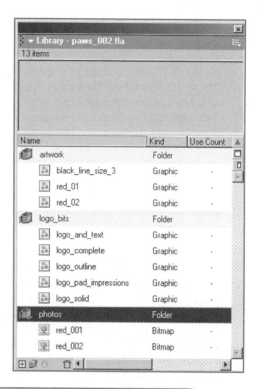

It is really important to make sure that you name your Flash assets so that you can easily work with them – if you come back to the file in six months to update it, you need to know where everything is.

5. Currently, the main timeline should look like the image shown. It's not that complex yet, but this is going to be our main site movie where everything will be controlled from, so we need to do some work. Add two new layers, and name them `labels` and `scripts`. Drag the `labels` layer so that it's at the top of the list of layers, and the `actions` layer so that it's just underneath the `labels` layer. These two layers will affect all the other layers, so it's important to have them at the top where we can see them.

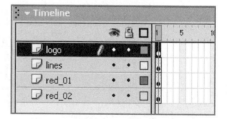

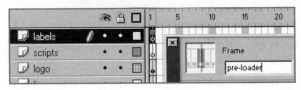

6. Later on, we're going to build a preloader (in Session 15, to be precise) to show the user something is happening while we load up the PAWS site, and we're going to put this in the first frame. So we can tell Flash to go to this, we need to add a label in the first frame of the `labels` layer. Select the first frame of the `labels` layer and look in your Property inspector. On the left-hand side, delete the `<frame label>` text and add `pre-loader`. You should now see a flag appear on the timeline to show the label (if you move your mouse over the frame for a second or two, the label name will appear in a handy tool tip).

7. Now select frame 10 in the `labels` layer. Hold down the SHIFT key, and click in frame 10 of the bottom layer. Frame 10 should now be highlighted in all your layers. Insert a blank keyframe (Insert > Blank Keyframe) into these. Now repeat this for frames 15, 20, 25, 30, 35, and 40.

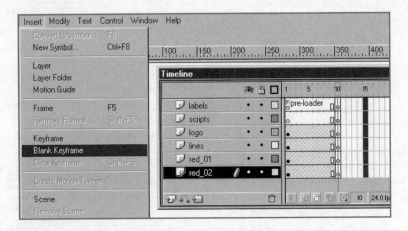

8. Add these labels to the corresponding frame in the `labels` layer. Make sure that for each you tick the `Named Anchor` box just underneath the label name in the Property inspector (as shown). You'll notice that we have gold anchors on the timeline instead of red flags to show that we have ticked the `Named Anchor` box. This will allow some users (mainly those with IE6 running in Windows) to use their back buttons when navigating around our site.

- frame 10 – home
- frame 15 – events
- frame 20 – animals
- frame 25 – gallery
- frame 30 – about
- frame 35 – contact

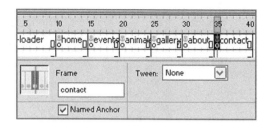

9. You may or may not have guessed that frame 10 (labeled home) is going to contain the main page of our site, from where the user can navigate to other pages. This being the case, we need to move the content that we had left on frame 1 onto frame 10. Select the first frame of logo, lines, red_01, and red_02 by clicking and then SHIFT-clicking as we did before. Click on the highlighted frames, and drag them across to frame 10, leaving frames 1-9 free for our pre-loader.

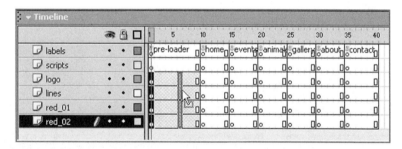

10. Some of the content is going to be the same for all sections of the site, so we can remove some of the keyframes we put in earlier. The logo, for example, will stay the same whichever page we're on. On the logo layer, click on frame 15, SHIFT-click on frame 40, and select Insert > Clear Keyframe. Do the same for the lines, red_01, and red_02 layers. Your timeline should now look like the one shown.

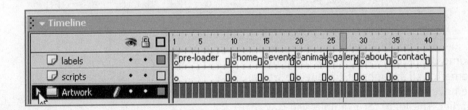

11. Earlier, we put some of our library content into a folder, and you can do exactly the same thing with layers. Insert a layer folder by clicking on the Insert Layer Folder icon just to the right of the Add Motion Guide icon at the bottom-left of the timeline.

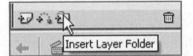

12. Name the folder Artwork. Drag the logo, lines, red_01, and red_02 layers into your new folder, so that all the generic artwork that we're going to display across all our pages is in one place. If it's not already, drag the folder so that it's underneath the scripts layer.

> *You'll see that you can display or hide the contents of the layer folder on the timeline by clicking on the little arrow button to the left of the folder.*

13. Now, add two more folders called content and navigation. In the navigation folder, add a layer called navBtns. In the content folder, add the following layers: events, animals, gallery, about, and contact. In each of the new layers inside the folders, put blank keyframes on frames 10, 15, 20, 25, 30, 35, and 40 as we did ear-

lier. (It's quickest if you make sure both
folders are next to each other and open,
and then use the SHIFT-click method.) Close
the folders and save the Flash file when
you've finished.

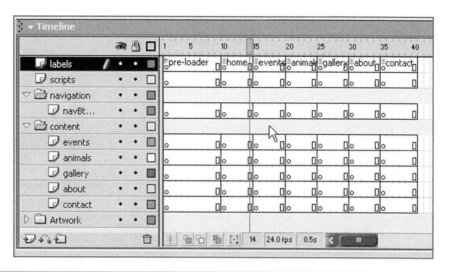

14. We're now going to do something that
unnecessarily scares some people: we're
going to add a tiny bit of **ActionScript** to
control our Flash movie. Don't worry: you
don't have to know anything to do this, and
it's not difficult at all. Select the frame
under the home label in the scripts layer,
and open up the **Actions** panel. It's quite
often nested above or below the Property
inspector, and you can just use the little
arrow to maximize it. If it's not there,
Window > Actions will do the trick.

15. Before we go any further, just above the top
right-hand corner of the white pane, click
on the View Options button, and make sure
that Normal Mode is checked. This makes

sure that Flash gives us a little bit of a help-
ing hand in adding our script.

16. The pane on the left of the Actions panel
contains all the Actions we could possibly
want. Click on the Actions book, and then
the Movie Control book.

17. Check that the keyframe in the scripts layer
just underneath the home label is still selected – it's very easy to put a script somewhere else with a random click. Double-
click on the stop action, and you should
see the stop(); command appear in the
white pane on the left. You'll also see a
small a appear in the frame on the timeline,
to indicate that you've attached a script to
this frame.

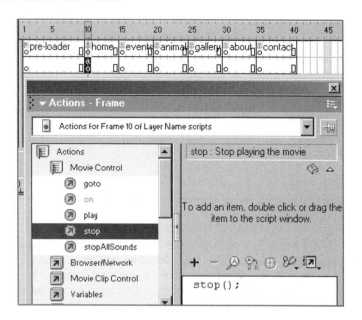

What does this do? Well, you should be able to work it out, and if not, the tool tip will tell you: it stops the timeline where it is. Flash won't carry on past this until we give it some further instructions. This is exactly what we want to happen on each of the pages of our site. We don't want Flash to show someone our home page for a few seconds, and then the upcoming events page for a few seconds, and so on, and then start all over again. We want it to go to a page and then stop, waiting for the user to tell it where to go next.

18. We'll deal with going to other pages in the next session. For now, we just want to stop everything, so add `stop();` actions in the `Actions` layer underneath the `events`, `animals`, `gallery`, `about`, and `contact` labels.

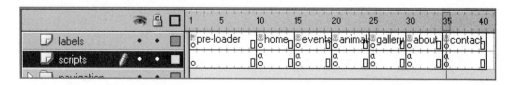

If you want some extra help with what an Action does, click on the little Arrow (if it is pointing down) to the right of the little book at the top right-hand corner of the Actions panel, underneath the Pin icon:

This will display a description of the Action at the top of the right-hand pane, as you can see in the screenshot for step 17.

Further Steps

This has been a tidying-up session, so there's not that much you can do with what you've learned here in isolation. What we've done here is incredibly important when you come to make your own sites, and will save you a lot of time, so don't forget about this. Take a break, and come back to the next session: we've got the basics out of the way, and laid a good foundation for our site, so we can start the much more exciting business of generating some content for the site.

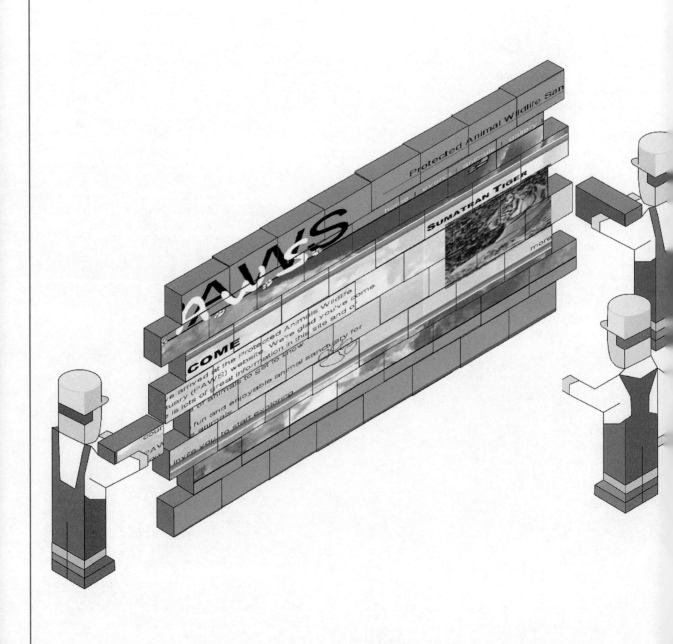

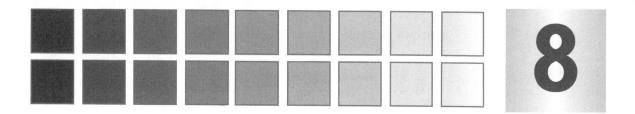

Navigation

In the last session, we set up our main Flash movie PAWS.fla so that it had a number of frame labels for the different parts of our site. In this session, we're going to set things up so that the user can easily navigate to different parts of the site.

This is a really important step, and often one that's tacked on at the end of a website design process. It's far more important than that, though: if people can't find the content they want from our site easily, then they're not going to stick around for long. We've all suffered the frustration of wandering around a site trying to find something, and finding different links and corners of the site at every step, and we don't want that here.

It's worth making a note here that because we are building the navigation on one layer across all frames, we are keeping a consistent navigation theme. This helps the user find and then use the navigation, rather than risking the user getting frustrated and leaving our site when they can't find what they are looking for.

We're going to provide navigation for our users by providing them with **buttons** to press in order to go to specific pages (you'll remember that we've set up labels for a preloader, our home page, and pages called events, animals, gallery, about and contact).

You create buttons in the same way as any other symbol in Flash: either by creating Insert > New Symbol, or by creating some content, selecting it, and using Insert > Convert to Symbol. You'll notice straight away with buttons that the timeline looks somewhat different to other symbols: it's just four frames, and these are called up, over, down, and hit.

These are the four **states** of a button:

- up is the button's default state, which the user will see when they first open the page.

- over is how the button looks as the mouse is over it.

- `down` is how the button looks when it's pressed (this state doesn't last for long, so it's best not to add any lengthy animations/effects to this state if you don't want to irritate your users too much).

- `hit` defines what area the mouse has to enter for the over and down states to display.

It is by no means necessary for a button to have something in every state. The simplest button is just a `Hit` state – which would, of course, be invisible to the user, as there would be nothing in the `Up` state. A button must have a `Hit` state, or else it won't work. Most buttons have at least a `Hit` state, and an `Up` state. The buttons we'll be creating will also have `Over` states, and will have more than one layer. Before we get too confused with all this theory, let's see how it all works...

1. Open your `PAWS_003.fla` (or use `PAWS_003` from the CD). The first thing we're going to do is add some dummy content, so that we know the navigation actually works. Add a new layer to the main timeline, and call it `dummy`. Move it so that it's above the `navigation` layer folder.

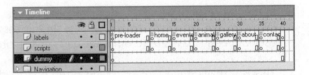

2. Add blank keyframes underneath each of the labels on the `labels` layer. Select the keyframe underneath the `home` label, and select the Text tool from your `Tools` panel. Don't worry about the font, but set the text size to something at least as big as 60, and the color to black. Make sure that you've still got the correct keyframe selected, and write `home` on the stage in between the two borders. Repeat this for the `events`, `animals`, `gallery`, `about`, and `contact` labels.

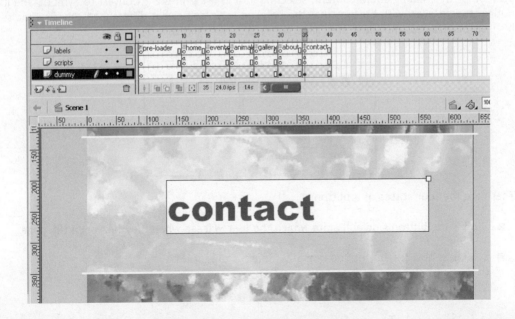

3. Drag the `Dummy` layer below the navigation folder. We need the dummy text layer to be underneath to make it easier to line the text up on top easier. This helps if you forget to lock the `Dummy` layer later.

4. Open the `Navigation` layer folder. Select frame 10 of the `navBtns` layer (which should line up with the `home` label), and re-select your Text tool, if it's not still selected from the last step. In your Property inspector, make sure this is set to `Static Text`, with a font of `_sans`, and a size of `12`. Type the following, with two spaces between each word and the | symbol:

> home | events | animals | gallery | about | contact

5. Select the Arrow tool instead of the Text tool, and select the text we've just created. Bring up the Info panel (Window > Info), and set the `X` and `Y` values to `X: 330` and `Y: 61`.

> *If you're working from your own files, remember that these locations won't work unless your Flash movie is set to a 640x480 size in Modify > Document.*

6. Lock the `dummy` layer so that we can't alter it, by clicking underneath the padlock icon next to the layer, as shown.

The dummy layer is now used for two purposes. Not only does it contain content to test our navigation scripts, but it also holds the "sentence" of text for the navigation. We

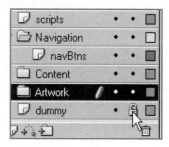

are now going to create the navigation
buttons and use the "sentence" in the
dummy layer to get the spacing and layout
correct. Later, once the buttons are lined up
correctly, and the navigation script is
working, we can then safely remove the
dummy layer in one shot.

7. Open the `navigation` folder. In the
   `navBtns` layer, we created in the last section, select the Text tool, and choose
   `Static Text`, with a font of `_sans`, and a
   size of `12` Click on the stage, and type
   `home`. Click somewhere else to create a different text box, and type `events`. Do the
   same for `animals`, `gallery`, `about`, `con-
   tact`, and `|`. We want these separate from
   each other, because we're going to turn
   them into buttons in a moment.

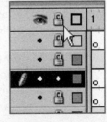

*If you hit the Padlock icon at the top, you'll notice that it locks all layers. If you
now unlock the navBtns layer by clicking on it, the other layers will remain
locked, making sure that you don't accidentally move any other items.*

8. Select the | character, and convert it to a graphic symbol called `pipe_graphic`. Now select each other bit of text individually, and convert them to button symbols with Insert > Convert to Symbol, just as you would convert something to a movie clip or graphic symbol. Call them: `home_btn`, `events_btn`, `animals_btn`, `gallery_btn`, `about_btn`, and `con-tact_btn`. Make sure the registration point for each is at the top left.

9. Select all of your new buttons, and use the Align panel (Window > Align) to line them up horizontally.

10. Select the `events` button and double-click it to edit it in place. Rename the default layer `text`. Add a keyframe to the `over` state, and add a blank keyframe to the `hit` state.

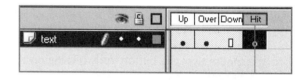

11. Select the `up` state, select the `events` text, and change the color from black to gray in the Property inspector. This sets the button up to initially appear gray, and then become black when we mouse over it.

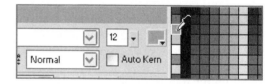

12. The hit state is going to be the area in which the user can press their mouse button to make the button work. If we left it now, as a lot of people do, the button will only work if the mouse is over a solid bit of text – if it's over the space in the n, hard luck. What we want to do is make a solid square area for the hit area. Select the `Hit` keyframe, and turn on Onion Skinning by clicking on the button at the bottom of the timeline, as shown. Make sure the markers go from the **over** state to the **hit** state

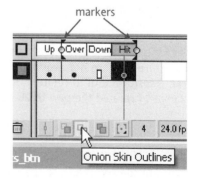

13. As you might have worked out, **onion skinning** allows you to see the contents of all the frames that you drag the markers out around. You can use it on any timeline, and

it's useful when you want to see the contents of other frames, in order to line things up. Here, we're using it to make sure that our hit area covers our text. Draw a rectangle to cover the text, and convert it to a graphic symbol called generic_square. Turn off the onion skins when you're done.

14. You may have seen **rollover** effects with buttons before – the button changes when a user's mouse passes over the button. These can be quite difficult and complex in normal web pages, but they're easy in Flash. Here, we're going to add the paw impressions graphic (in a slightly different place) to each button. To hold this, add a new layer to your button, and call it impression. Add keyframes to the Over and Hit states – we only want the effect when the user has their mouse over the button, or is clicking on the button.

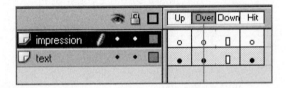

15. Select the Over state keyframe that you've just added, and drag an instance of logo_pad_impressions from the library and on to the stage. It will be huge, so bring up the transform palette (Window > Transform), and alter the graphic's size to 10% in both directions.

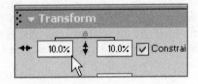

16. Place the resized graphic above the text, but make sure they are not overlapping. Use the Free Transform tool to rotate it. In my example, I rotated the paw to 26 degrees.

17. Save your file and return to the main timeline. Repeat steps 10-16 for each of the rest of the buttons, using your generic_square graphic from the library for the hit area (you'll need to use the Free Transform tool to scale it so that it fits the text snugly). Try the rotations for the logo_pad_impres-

sions graphic: 6, 31, 24, 57 degrees for the paw impressions, with 26 degrees for the paw impression in the home button.

18. Save your file, return to the main stage and test the movie. Run your mouse over the buttons to see if they work. You should see the cursor change, the text change color and the pad impression appear. Now that we have our buttons, the next step is to wire them up, so that pressing them makes something happen!

19. Select the home button, and open the Actions window (Window > Actions, or maximize it from underneath your Property inspector, if it's there). Just below the title bar across the top, check that the Actions panel is referring to your button. Now click on the Actions book in the left-hand pane, and then on the Movie Control book.

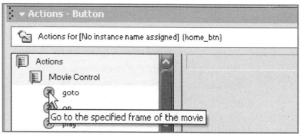

20. Double-click on the goto command - we want this button to tell our movie to goto our label. Your window will now look like this: it has created the script for you, and gives you three drop-down boxes that we can use to customize this action to do exactly what we want it to.

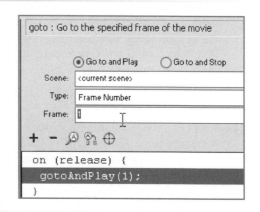

21. Click the drop-down menu that currently shows a choice of Frame Number, and change it to Frame label. Flash will now give us a choice of all the labels that it finds on the timeline, so select Home from the drop-down. When it gets to Home, we want Flash to stop where it is, not carry on playing along the timeline, so check the Go to and Stop radio button at the top.

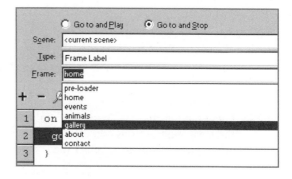

22. Check that you can see the pictured ActionScript in the right pane of your Actions window. Those of you who have used JavaScript in the past might recognize some of Flash's way of working things out here, but this script simply means:

```
on (release) {
  gotoAndStop("home");
}
```

when(the user presses the button), go to the label "home" and stop there

> As you've probably noticed, for ActionScript to work, every line of code **must** end with a semi-colon ;

23. We've set our button to send us to the home label when the user releases their mouse button, but we can change this. I'd prefer that the user is sent to home as soon as they press their mouse button, not as soon as they release it. Select the on(release) { line, and you'll see some options appear, as shown. Un-check the Release option, and check the Press option. We've now added some ActionScript to our button to control our Flash movie, and it really is as simple as that.

Event: ☑ Press
        ☐ Release
        ☐ Release Outside
        ☐ Key Press: [   ]

```
on (press) {
  gotoAndStop("home");
}
```

24. Select the events button, and open the Actions window. Follow steps 15-21 again, but this time select the Events label. Do the same for the animals, gallery, about and contacts buttons.

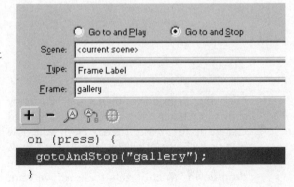

○ Go to and Play   ● Go to and Stop
Scene: <current scene>
Type: Frame Label
Frame: gallery

```
on (press) {
  gotoAndStop("gallery");
}
```

25. If you look at the timeline, you'll see that the navigation buttons currently only exist in the home frame area. Select the frames in

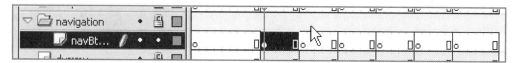

the `navBtn` layer from the `events` frame through to the `contact` frame, and choose Insert > Clear Keyframe.

26. What we've just done is make sure all of our buttons are available to all of the pages. There's one slightly untidy factor to take care of here, though. We don't really want the `home` button to be visible when we're already on the `home` page, do we? Add a keyframe to the `navBtn` layer under the `events` label. Now go back to the buttons on the `navBtn` layer under the `home` label, and delete the `home` button, and the first | symbol.

27. Save your file, test it, and check all the buttons work.

Further steps: controlling audio

We're going to add some sound controllers for the audio file we created earlier, using what we've just learned.

1. Open up the `audio.fla` file from Session 6. Add another three layers to the main timeline, and call them `Scripts`, `Labels`, and `btns`. Add a blank keyframe in the second frame of both `Scripts` and `Labels` layers.

2. Select the first frame of the `labels` layer, and use the Property inspector to label it `audio_on`. Select the second frame, and add the label `audio_off`.

> *No need to select the **named anchors** for these ones, as it's only going to be Action Script talking to these frames.*

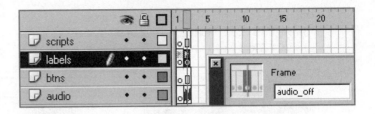

3. Select the Text tool, and choose Static Text, and _sans, size 12. In the `btns` layer, type `turn background audio |` `on` onto the stage. Turn on the **rulers** with View > Rulers. Click on the top ruler and drag a guide down to the 410 mark. Line the text up with the guide so that it's X and Y positions are `488,410`.

This might seem like a long way down, but we're putting them here so that they're underneath the rest of our site when we bring everything together later.

4. Add a keyframe in frame 2 of the `btns` layer, and change the `on` text to `off`. In the same way as with the buttons we made earlier turn the text on both keyframes into buttons, with gray text initially and black text when you roll over them, and a suitable hit area. Call these buttons `audio_on` and `audio_off`.

Creating these buttons is fairly simple – just follow these steps:

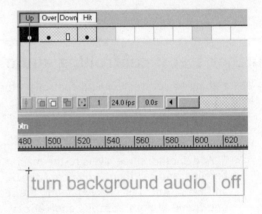

5. As we did in the last session, add `stop()`; actions to both the keyframes in the `Actions` layer (the `stop()`; action can be found under the `Actions` book, in the same `Movie Control` section as the `goto` actions we added earlier). Without these two stop actions, Flash would continually circle through the timeline, and our two buttons would flash on and off – the stop actions make sure that it stops on our buttons, until we tell it do to something else.

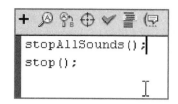

6. As you can probably guess, our on and off buttons are going to direct Flash to frame 1 (where the sound is) and frame 2 (where there is no sound). If your sound does exist in frames 1 and 2, then make sure you press F7 to insert a blank keyframe into frame 2 in the audio layer. There's one problem: because we set our sound to `Event` in Session 6, the sound will start playing when we tell it to, and keep playing. So, when we send Flash to frame 2, the sound will keep playing. To stop the sound from playing in frame 2, select the second frame of the `Actions` layer. Select the same Movie Control book (under Actions) from the left pane as before, and this time select `stopAllSounds`. This should go before the `stop` action – if it comes up after, select it with your mouse, and click on the up arrow at the right-hand corner of the right-hand pane, until the `stopAllSounds` line is at the top.

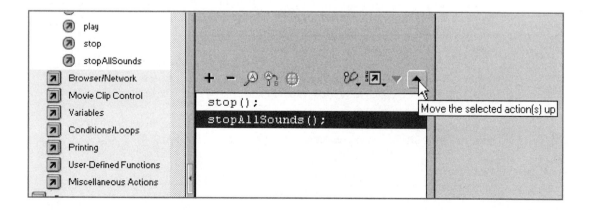

7. All that remains for us to do is follow steps 15-19 of the last exercise to add goto actions to the buttons. This time, the off text needs to go to the `audio_off` label on frame 2, and the on text needs to go to the `audio_on` label on the first frame. Your Actions windows should look like this:

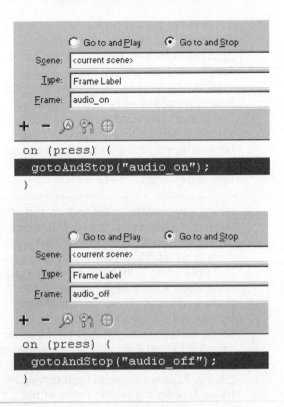

```
on (press) {
  gotoAndStop("audio_on");
}
```

```
on (press) {
  gotoAndStop("audio_off");
}
```

8. Save, and test your movie to check that your audio buttons work.

This has been a long session, and we've covered a lot in it, so reward yourself with a rest before going onto the next one. We've got our buttons and navigation working nicely now, so we'll start to replace that dummy text and create some proper pages for our buttons to navigate to in the next session.

> *Throughout this chapter we have created all of our navigational buttons as button symbols, which has been the traditional Flash way. Flash MX, however, allows us to create buttons as movie clip symbols, we then add in our own versions of the Up Over Down and Hit states using ActionScript.*
>
> *The beauty of this method is that it allows for a lot more flexibility than the button symbol method, you can have more than the four main states and you can incorporate all the extras that you'd expect in any movie clip – like embedded video or sound etc.*
>
> *At this stage, however, it is best to use the button symbols, but bear in mind the movie clip facility for when you have really got to grips with Flash MX.*

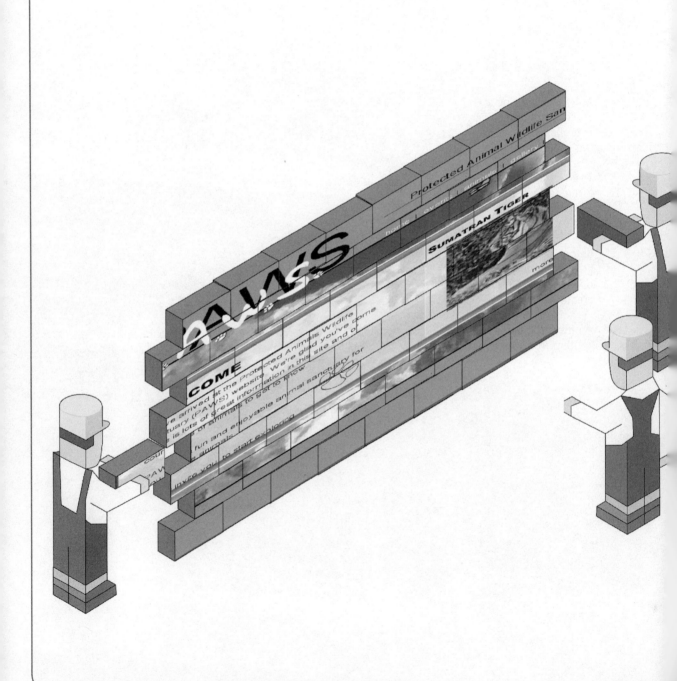

Adding simple content

A website with no content is no good at all, so we're going to spend this session adding some much needed detail to our site, now that the navigation is up and working well. Adding content is probably the most important aspect of building a website, so this session will be longer than the others in the book.

The session is split along the same lines as the pages we want our site to have – these will be included in our main Flash movie in the first two cases, but in a separate Flash movie for the `animals` page. This is because the `animals` page will include photos of the animals, and we don't want to force the user to wait for these to load up when they view the main home page.

Before we go ahead, let's look at the concept of **instantiation** in Flash. This basically means giving an individual occurrence of an instance its own name. In this session, we'll be using several different **instance names**, so that in future sessions we can refer back accurately to what we create here.

An **instance name** is a unique id for that occurrence of the symbol on the stage. When you drag an item from the Library onto the stage, Flash gives you an option to give it an **instance name**.

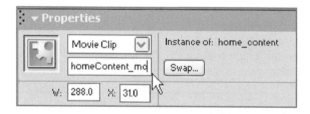

If you drag a movie clip out of the Library and onto the stage, and then drag another copy of that movie clip onto the stage next to it, then you'll have two identical copies of the movie clip. If you give them both different instance names, however, then you can use ActionScript to tell one of the movie clips to do something, whilst the other one stays still.

For example, I've been telling you to place particular items on the stage at specific x and y positions. ActionScript allows us to tell movie clips to move to particular locations. If we had a movie clip called `jim`, and we dragged two copies of `jim` out of the Library and onto the main stage, we could give the first an instance name of `bob_mc`. Now, if we wanted to move `bob_mc`, we could refer to him with some script. If we wanted to move our instance, we could use the ActionScript `_x` to change his x position on the stage like this:

```
bob_mc._x = 354;
```

In the example above, why didn't we just call the instance `bob`, rather than `bob_mc`? Flash will recognize what your instance name refers to and give you some handy hints in the code window if you name your instances according to their type in this way, `instanceName_type`. The following are a few of the types:

- `_mc` denotes a movie clip (`roundBall_mc`, for example)
- `_btn` denotes a button (`blueSquare_btn`, for example)
- `_txt` denotes a text object (`content_txt`, for example)

It's particularly important to name your instance names well, as misspelling one of these in a script is a surefire way to make sure that things don't work.

The home page

1. Open up the `paws.fla` that you've been working on, or open up `paws_004.fla` from the CD. Collapse all the layer folders, and delete the `dummy` layer by CTRL/right-clicking and selecting Delete Layer.

2. Open the `content` folder, and add a new layer called `home` to it. Add keyframes under the `home` and `events` labels. Lock all other layers apart from this one, so that we don't go adding content anywhere else.

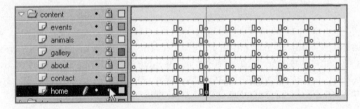

3. Select the first keyframe on our `home` layer, and enter some welcome text. Position this on the left-hand side of the white area. I've used `_sans`, size 12 to fit in with the rest of the site, and the text shown in the screenshot. Give the text X and Y values of 33 and

185 in the Info window, and choose the Multiline option, instead of the Single Line option from the drop-down menu in the Property inspector (this might not make much difference here, but it will when Flash tries to display each paragraph as a single line!).

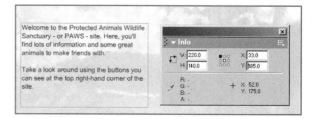

4. Add a title in size 30 _sans, and position this above the text you've just entered. Either turn on the rulers with View > Rulers, or select both pieces of text by SHIFT-clicking and use the Align window to line both bits of text up with each other.

5. To add a little visual touch, drag an instance of logo_outline out of logo.fla's library and onto the stage. As usual, it'll be huge, so bring up the Transform panel, and reduce it to a size of 10%. Whilst in the Transform panel, enter a rotation value of 30 degrees to move the logo around to the right a little. Position this at the bottom right-hand corner of your text, and we use Modify > Break Apart to break it apart.

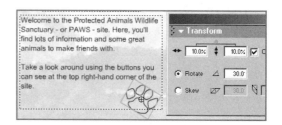

6. Select your text, the title, and the logo, and convert it to a movie clip called home_content with the registration point at top left as usual. In the Property inspector, give it the instance name homeContent_mc.

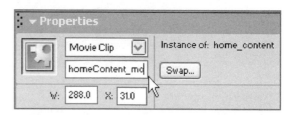

The events page

1. Unlock the event layer, and lock the home layer. On the event layer, select the keyframe underneath the event label, and enter Events @ PAWS in the same bold _sans, size 30 that we used for our Welcome heading. It's important that the user can find the headings on our different pages easily, so unlock the home layer a moment, and note down the X and Y values for the Welcome heading. Select the Events @ PAWS text, and enter the same values into the Info Window.

2. Now we want to set up the area to contain the text describing our events. We're going to do this a little differently to the text on the home page, as we're probably going to want to update this section quite often. It's going to be a pain to open Flash up and change everything in Flash, and then create new SWFs and so on every time we want to update things: it's even possible that you (or the person updating the site) won't always have access to a full version of Flash. So, we're going to set this up to load in text from a simple .txt file stored in the same place as the Flash file. This way, you'll only have to alter the .txt file to update things. To do this, make sure you have the Text tool selected, and change the first drop-down box in your Property inspector from Static Text to Dynamic Text.

3. Change the Single Line option to Multiline (if you can't see this option, expand your Property inspector in the usual way), and make sure the Selectable icon immediately

to the right of the Multiline drop-down is selected. Now, draw a text box underneath your title large enough to fit your news – mine is about 350 by 150. Use the Align window to align the title up with the text box.

4. As soon as you've drawn the box, the Property inspector will allow you to add an instance name to your text box: enter textScroll and double-check that you've spelt this right: a simple mistake here will cause a lot of trouble later on when we try and load the text in. At the same time, make sure you've selected the Multiline option, and you've changed the size of the font from the size 30 we used for the heading to 12.

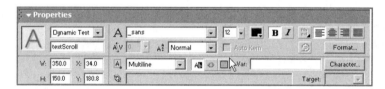

5. Chances are that, if we're loading in our events from a text file, we're going to find it very difficult to guess what will fit exactly in that box each time. We could just spend ages testing different text documents until they fit each time... or we could save ourselves a lot of hassle and add a scrollbar to the box, so no matter how much text we add, we can scroll down to see it. In previous versions of Flash, scrollbars required a fair bit of tricky coding, but Flash MX comes with a number of pre-built useful Flash elements for us, including a scrollbar. These are called **components**, and you can see what's available by going to Window > Components now.

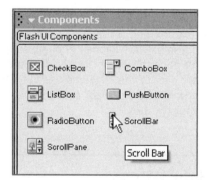

The components you will see here are the Flash UI Components installed as standard: you can find details on installing further components at Macromedia's Exchange (http://www.macromedia.com/exchange/), and in the forthcoming friends of ED book Flash MX Components Most Wanted (http://www.friendsofed.com).

6. Drag the scrollbar component onto the stage, and make sure you drag it actually into the text box before releasing the mouse button as close to the edge as you can. If you look in the Property inspector now, you should see that the scrollbar's instance name is set to `textScroll`. It's this instance name which we'll use in session 16 to tell Flash where to load our text file into.

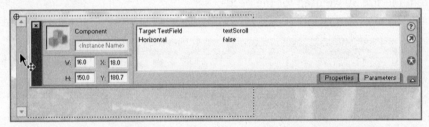

7. The scrollbar should snap to the edge of the text box, and resize itself automatically. This doesn't always happen, though, so if it hasn't done this automatically, drag the scrollbar over to the edge and use the Info window to set the height to the same value as your text box.

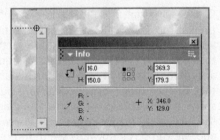

The animals page

We've placed the content for the home and events pages straight into our main FLA, but we're going to place the content for our other pages into external files for Flash to load in. This means that our main FLA will load quicker, and those users on slow connections won't get too bogged down waiting for things to display. A few short waits is a lot better than one long wait, especially when users can choose what they do and don't want to wait for.

1. Create a new Flash movie. Go to Modify > Document, and set the dimensions of your movie to 640x216. This is exactly the size of the white area in the middle of the main FLA. Save this as `animal_content.fla`.

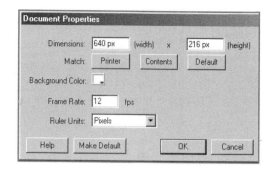

2. Rename the default layer `backing`, and add six new layers. Starting at the top, rename these: `scripts`, `labels`, `navigation`, `menuBtns`, `menuText`, and `content`.

3. We're going to use scripts to jump to labels on our timeline, as we did in the last session. We're going to add provision for seven animals here, though you could always add more. In the `labels` layer, add keyframes and labels to these frames:

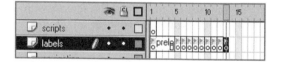

       1 – `preloader`
       5 – `menu`
       6 – `tiger`
       7 – `ringtail`
       8 – `panda`
       9 – `lion`
       10 – `giraffe`
       11 – `rhino`
       12 – `tortoise`
       13 – `end`

4. In the `scripts` layer, add keyframes to frames 5 and 13. Add a `stop();` action to the first, and `gotoAndStop("menu");` to the second – check back to the last section if you've forgotten how to add these.

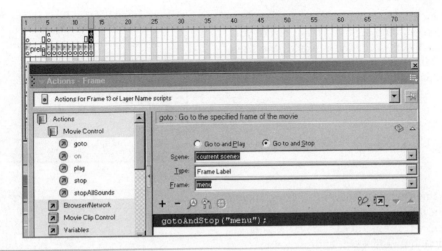

5. In the `content` layer, add a keyframe to frame 5. Into this, enter some text, using the standard text settings of _sans, size 12. Make sure it's set to Static Text, after our Dynamic Text adventures earlier. You can see what I've used in the screenshot. Place the text on the left of the screen, with enough room above it for a title.

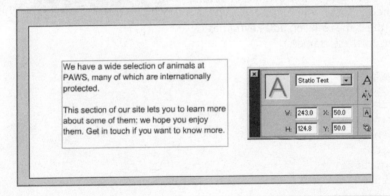

6. Enter the title `Animals @ PAWS` in capitals, using the usual bold _ sans font, but with the slightly smaller size of 28, so that it fits. Use the Align window to line up the left-hand side of the text box with the title text.

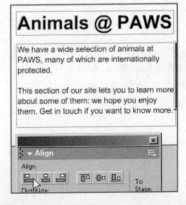

7. Select the `menutext` layer, and add a keyframe at frame 5. On this, type the following, using the traditional `_sans`, but size 15 this time: `tiger; ring tailed lemur; red panda; african lions; giraffe; white rhino; giant tortoise`. Add a line break between each animal, and drag the text box to the right hand-side of your screen, so that it fits nicely with the intro text that we've added.

8. Instead of making individual buttons for each of these, we're going to cheat and make one invisible button that will work for them all. On the `menu_btns` layer, add keyframes at frame 5 and frame 6. In frame 5, draw a rectangle without a stroke to cover the `ring tailed lemur` text on the `menuBtns` layer, by clicking on the No Color button under Stroke on the Colors panel, as shown.

9. Convert this rectangle to a graphic symbol called `generic_rectangle`, and convert the graphic symbol to a button called `invs_btn`.

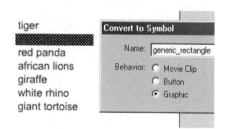

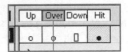

10. Double-click on this button to edit it in place. Click on the keyframe in the Up state, and drag it across to the Hit state. Because there's nothing in the Up, Over, or Down states, the user cannot see the button itself. It will still behave exactly like a button, though – when the user's mouse hovers over it, the cursor will change to indicate that it's a button, and we can attach Actions to it to take the user somewhere when the button is clicked. An invisible button will show up as cyan in Flash, so that you can see where to locate them – don't worry, the user viewing your SWF won't be able to see this.

11. To let our users know that they are rolling over a button, place a keyframe in the Over state. In this, add a line under the text using the Line tool set to Hairline in the Property inspector.

12. We now have a generic button that we can scale to fit each of the animal names. Go back to the main timeline and drag a copy of the button out of the library for each of our seven animals. Use the Free Transform tool to scale the button instances to fit each of the names. (You'll find this a lot easier if you use View > Zoom In to zoom in a few times so that you can fit the buttons to the text precisely.)

13. Click on the tiger button and open the Actions window. Add a goto action, as we have before, and specify the tiger frame label. Check the gotoAndStop radio button, and change the initial mouse action to press instead of release. Add similar actions pointing to the matching labels for each of the buttons.

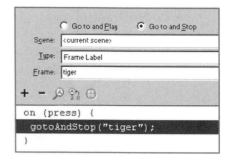

14. Select File > Import to Library, and choose the images in the `Photos` directory on the CD: `giant_tortoise_01.jpg`, `giraffe_rhino_01.jpg`, `lion_sleep_02.jpg`, `ringtail_01.jpg`, and `tiger_01.jpg`. We've an image for each of the animals except for the giraffe and rhino, who share a photo, but that's okay – helps keep the file size down. Once you've imported the images, create a new folder in the library, and move them there to keep things tidy.

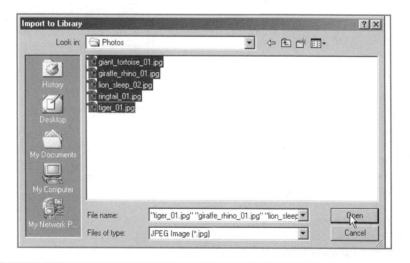

15. Add a blank keyframe to the `content` layer under the `tiger` label. Drag the `tiger_01` picture out of the library and into this keyframe. Select it on the stage, and convert it to a graphic symbol called `tiger_01`, with the registration point in the center this time. Use the Transform window to scale it to 60% so that it fits into the Flash movie.

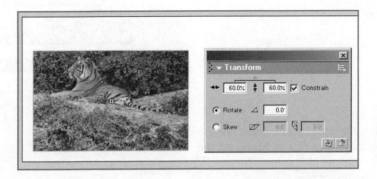

16. Add a title – Sumatran Tiger - in size 20 _sans font, and use the Align window to line it up with the left-hand side of the tiger.

17. Create a Dynamic text box for some descriptive text about the tiger, in the same way as we did before: choose the Text tool and select Dynamic Text in the Property inspector. Set this to Multiline, but – unlike last time – make sure that the Selection button, immediately to the right of the Multiline option, isn't selected. We might have wanted people to be able to copy event times and details if they wanted, but we'd like to keep our information from being copied. Draw your text box next to our tiger picture, and give it the instance name of tiger_info.

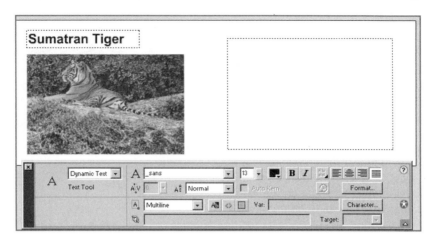

18. Open up the Components window again, and drag a scrollbar component into this text box. Check that it picks up the `tiger_info` instance name by checking in the Property inspector.

19. Open the `Sumatran Tiger Document.rtf` file from the CD in your text editor of choice. Copy the text and paste it into your text box in Flash. Turn it into 12 point `_sans`. Save and test your movie – click on the tiger button, and it should move to the tiger section, complete with scrollable text.

Sumatran Tiger

The Sumatran Tiger

The Sumatran is the smallest of the tiger species. It is known for its reddish orange hide with narrow black, gray or brown stripes. Tigers have muscular front legs with large paws armed with sharp claws. They have strong back legs which are used for pouncing on their prey. Males can grow to a length of

20. Insert keyframes in the `content` layer under each of the frame labels. On each of the new keyframes, delete the picture,

insert the relevant picture from the Library, and turn it into a graphic symbol. Alter the text titles accordingly, and change the instance name in the Property inspector for both the text box and the scrollbar to: `ringtail_info`, `redPanda_info`, `lion_info`, `giraffe_info`, `rhino_info`, `tortoise_info`. You will need to use the Transform window, or the Free Transform tool, to scale a few of the images so that they fit snugly, and you'll find that – at present – we have no information on the Panda, so enter some place holding "information coming soon" text there.

Red Panda

The animals page navigation

We need to allow the user some way to go somewhere after they've looked at our descriptions – whether that's back to the menu, or onto another animal.

1. Create a keyframe on the `navigation` layer under the `tiger` label. In this keyframe, create a rectangle with no stroke and use the Property inspector to make it 640 x 12 pixels in size.

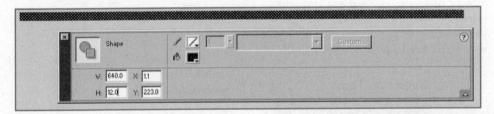

2. Create a gradient for this shape that starts at a deep gray, fades to light and then quickly back to deep gray, similar to the gradient shown here:

3. Use the Color Mixer to create your gradient , just as we did in session 4. Here's a lightning speed recap on how to mix custom gradients. To adjust the color, you can slide the gradient

stops up and down the gradient bar, you can add new gradient stops by clicking under the gradient bar, and remove stops by dragging them away,. You can change the color of a selected stop by clicking in the color chip at the top of the Color Mixer.

3. Once you are happy with your gradient, you can save it by clicking the triangle in the top right-hand corner of the Color Mixer, and choose Add Swatch from the drop-down menu. This gradient will now be available in the Swatches panel for this movie. Zoom in, and use your cursor keys to position this across the very bottom of the stage, and convert it to a movie clip called base_nav.

4. Double-click on base_nav to edit it in place, and rename the default layer base. Insert a keyframe in frame 5. In frame 1, move the movie clip vertically down and off the stage. In your Property inspector, set the Tween drop-down to Shape, so that base_nav will move from its new location to the original location (in frame 5) gradually.

5. Add two new layers called actions and btns, and add a blank keyframe in frame 5 of both layers. Bring up the Actions window for frame 5 of the actions layer, and add a stop(); action.

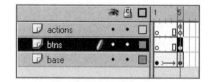

6. In frame 5 of the btns layer, type next in size 12 with Arial Black font. Color the text white, and position this towards the right-hand side of the bar, as shown. Convert it to a button called next_btn. Add a little arrow to the right of the next

text – create it by drawing two short lines, hold down SHIFT to constrain the lines to 45 degree angles.

7. Double-click on your new button to edit it. You may want to zoom in to get a good view of what's going on with your button here. Insert a keyframe in the Over state, and a blank keyframe in the Hit state. In the Hit state, turn on onion skinning, as we have previously, and draw a rectangle around the text.

8. Repeat steps 25 to 26 to create a previous_btn button that faces the other way and sits on the other side of the stage. Finally, create a return_btn button that sits in the middle and reads return to full list. These should all reside on frame 5 of the btns layer in your base_nav movie clip.

9. The Next button is going to tell the main timeline to go to the next frame (remember, all our pictures and information are on successive keyframes). Select the button, and bring up the Actions window. In the left-hand pane of your Actions window, click on the Objects book, and then go to Movie > Movie Clip > Methods. You should now be able to double-click on nextFrame. (If you really can't find it, then go to the last book – Index – which has an alphabetical list of all actions, and choose it from here.)

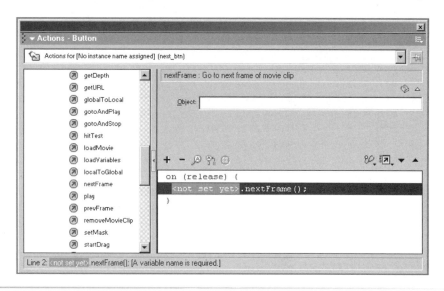

10. Your actions window should now show your .nextFrame action, with an on (release) above it, as Flash has detected we're working with a button here. There's also a big red <not set yet> bit of text before .nextFrame, and this is because we need to tell Flash what we want it to go to the next frame. If we think carefully about it, we don't want Flash to go to the next frame of our base_nav movie clip, because it won't get anywhere – it only has five frames, and we're on frame 5 already. What we actually want it to do is to go to the next frame of our main timeline. Our movie clip is on our main timeline, and in Flash ActionScript, going back up one timeline in the hierarchy of nesting is done using _parent.

11. In the Objects > Movie section in the left pane, you should see _parent just below the Movie Clip book that we've been in. Click once in Object box, just above the main script pane, so that your cursor appears in it, and then double-click on _parent.

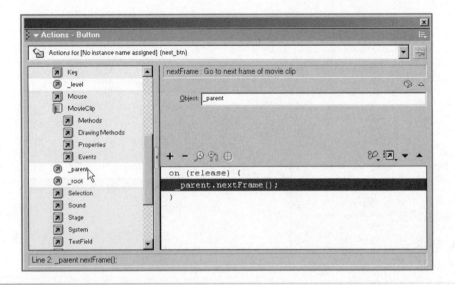

12. We've got the other buttons to do now. For the Previous button, we want exactly what the Next button had, but using prevFrame instead of nextFrame. You can find this in exactly the same place as nextFrame, so I'll leave you to follow the last two steps to achieve this code:

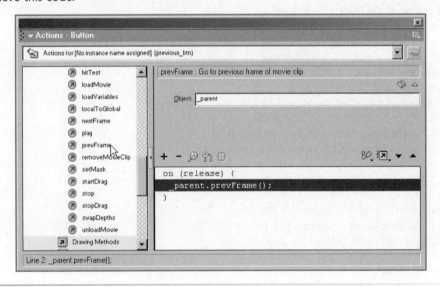

13. For the return to full list button, we want to add a gotoAndPlay("menu"); command. Because the menu label that we

want it to go to is on the main timeline,
though, we need to add the `_parent` first,
so do that now.

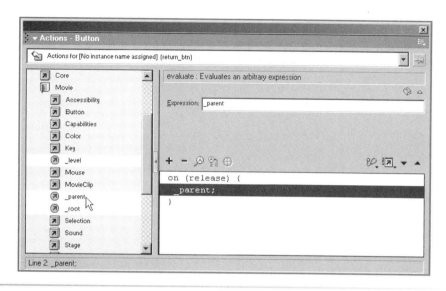

14. In the box above the main script pane that
says `Expression:`, type a . (full stop)
immediately after `_parent`. A menu will
immediately appear, from which you can
choose `gotoAndPlay`. You then need to finish this off by telling it where we want it to
go to on our main timeline – `main` – and
add a closing bracket, so that you have
`_parent.gotoAndPlay("main");` displayed in the `Expression:` box.

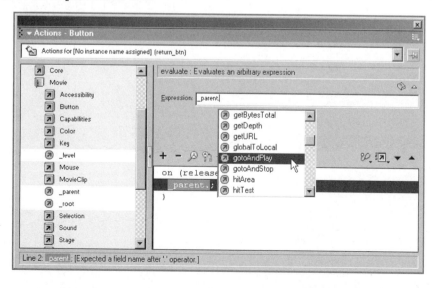

15. Save your movie and test it, and you should
find your new navigation system working
nicely.

This session has been a long one, but we've covered a lot of ground here, we've looked at the basics of
adding simple content to our site, either straight into the FLA or as external files for Flash to load in. In
the next session, we'll discover how to add a video to our animals page.

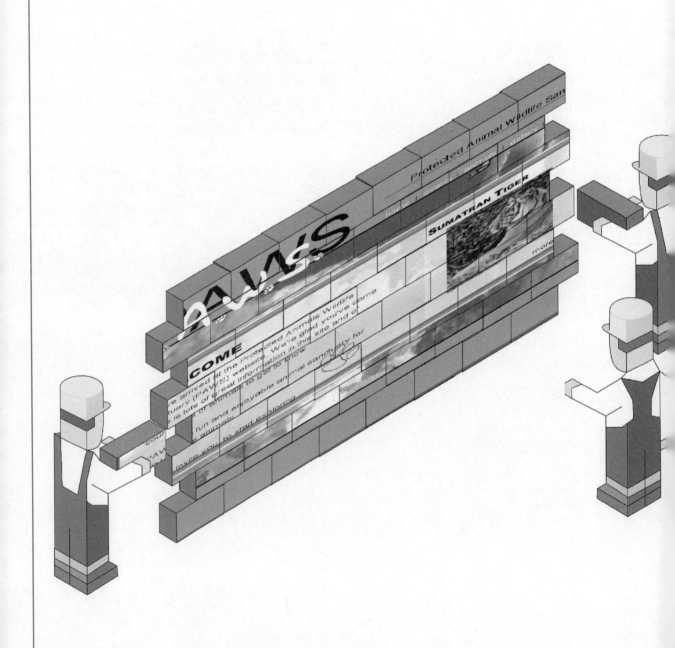

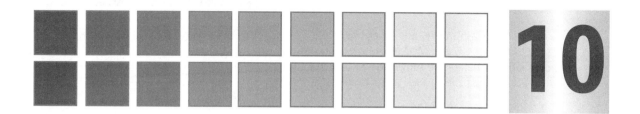

Adding video

One of the great things about Flash MX is that, for the first time, it includes full support for displaying video content as standard. Before Flash MX, putting video on the web was tricky, because people needed a separate plug-in to their browser to view the video, and this plug-in is usually a substantial download. With Flash, all you need is the Flash plug-in, and this is small and easy to download.

As with sound, the next question to ask is: from where do we get our footage? Well, you've probably noticed the increase in sales of digital video cameras, which will load your recorded video onto your computer for you to edit as you like. In addition, still digital cameras – even those towards the bottom end of the market – often allow for the capture of thirty second or so video clips.

> *If you want to find out more about Digital Video and Digital Photography, then friends of ED have a range of books to help you. Check out the friends of ED site for titles like Flash MX Video, and Digital Photography with Photoshop Elements 2.*

As with sound, if you don't have the equipment – or, in our case, an available tiger to film – there are plenty of places that have video clips for sale. Unlike sounds and images, you'll probably have a harder time finding free footage, so it's worth finding a friend with a camera if you're going to do this often.

We loaded the animal content Flash movie into a separate Flash movie to save the user from having to download everything at once, and we're following the same theory here. To make sure that the video, which is a fairly hefty 322kb, is only loaded if required, we're going to create a Flash movie to hold our video file here, and then load that file separately into our animal content movie.

1. Create a new Flash movie, and save it as `tiger_video.fla`. Use Modify > Document to change the movie to `182x162`, and set the `Frame Rate` to 24fps.

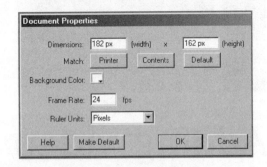

2. Rename the default layer `frame`. On this, select the Rectangle tool, and click on the `Round Rectangle Radius` button in the Options panel on the left. In the Rectangle Settings window that then appears, set the Corner Radius to 3 points to give our rectangle some nicely curved corners.

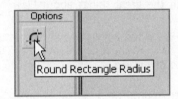

3. Turn off the fill, and then draw a rectangle so that it fits around your stage perfectly.

4. Insert three more layers, and call them `scripts`, `buttons`, and `video`. As usual, drag the `scripts` layer up to the top. On the video layer, create a new movie clip called `tiger_movie`. Double-click this to edit it in place, and rename the default layer `video`.

5. Import `tiger2ss.mov` from the CD by going to File > Import, this will cause the Import Video window to open. For our website you should opt to embed the video in your Flash document, but there may well be

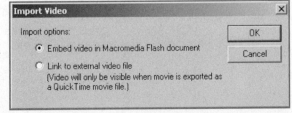

occasions when you would choose to link to
an external video file.

> *The option to link to an external video file is only available when importing
> QuickTime movies. It is a useful import method to use when presenting a video in
> its original form. The benefit of importing video in this way is that the FLA itself
> does not contain the video file; instead the video is loaded when it is called upon.
> The downside to this method is that the Flash content needs to be exported in
> Flash 4.*

6. The Import Video Settings window will then
open. As you can see from this, Flash makes
use of the Sorenson Spark **codec** to import
and compress video. (Codec is short for
compressor – decompressor, which is
what Spark does for you – compresses the
video so that it's nice and small for the user
to download, and then decompresses it so
that they can view it.)

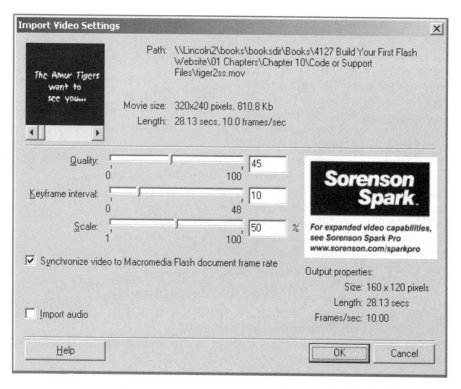

You may also hear people refer to Sorenson Squeeze. This is a very much more powerful version of Spark, available for you to buy from Sorenson (www.sorenson.com). Spark is fine for our purposes here, but if you're planning on doing more with video, you may want to take a look at Squeeze.

7.   There are quite a few options on this screen and once you've set them Spark creates the video content for Flash (at this point the video is stored as an FLV movie clip inside Flash's library). You will have to come back and create another version of the file if you want to change anything, so we'll now run through each setting to make sure we've got things right.

First up is `Quality`, which adjusts the amount of compression we're applying to our video – just like the JPEG quality setting we dealt with in session 3. We're scaling the video to half the original size, so we can get away with quite a bit here: set it to 45.

KeyFrame Interval is an important setting, as it determines the number of keyframes in the clip. This setting works with the Quality setting to determine what your movie will look like. Each keyframe will hold the complete data for a frame, whilst Sorenson Spark will approximate for the frames in between keyframes. A setting of 40 will place a keyframe at every fortieth frame; a setting of 30 will place a keyframe in every thirtieth frame and so on. The lower the number you set here, the more keyframes, the higher the quality and the higher the file size. Set this to 10.

`Scale` is a little easier to understand – it sets the size of the movie clip. Set this to 50% - this will make our video smaller, and our file size smaller.

`Synchronize` is an important setting. Look

at the top of the Import Video Settings window and you'll see that the frame rate of our original video clip is 10 frames per second, but remember that we set our Flash document to 24 frames per second. If we let this go ahead, then the video would play slower than intended, so check this box to tell Sorenson to play the video at 24fps. Sorenson attempts to pack the same content across 24 frames by dropping the extra frames– so the content that is in a particular frame in MOV may not be in FLV. There is a risk that by dropping the extra frames our video will have a choppier effect, but as we are only losing 6 frames per second it will not have a huge impact on our final piece. Sorenson doesn't simply rip out the extra frames, but rather resamples the content to 24 fps.

Uncheck the Import Audio box, so that we don't import sound that will interfere with our site soundtrack. Check the bottom right-hand corner to see a summary of our Output properties. Compare it with the details at the top, and you should see that we've adjusted the size from 320x240 to 160x120 by setting the scale to 50%, we've adjusted the frame rate to 24fps, and the length of the clip is the same. Press OK to import the video, and wait for Spark to work its magic.

Once Spark has finished, it'll place the video on the timeline of the movie clip we had open when we went to import our video. It'll work out how many frames on the timeline it needs to exactly play the video, and then prompt you to ask if it's OK to add these frames. Click OK, and it'll add these.

8. Return to the main timeline, and open your library. It should have two items in it. The one with the little digital camera icon is the embedded video clip. You will see in the timeline that Flash has placed your video on

Movie size: 320x240 pixels, 6208.3 Kb
Length: 16.43 secs, 30.0 frames/sec

☑ Synchronize video to Macromedia Flash document frame rate

Output properties:
Size: 160 x 120 pixels
Length: 16.43 secs
Frames/sec: 24.00

☐ Import audio

Help

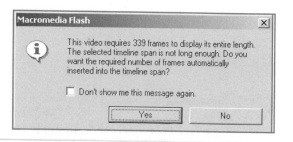

Macromedia Flash

ⓘ This video requires 339 frames to display its entire length. The selected timeline span is not long enough. Do you want the required number of frames automatically inserted into the timeline span?

☐ Don't show me this message again.

Yes   No

tiger_movie   Movie Clip
tiger2ss.mov   Embedded …

the stage and created 339 frames to contain the video.

9. Drag an instance of `tiger_movie` movie clip out of the Library and onto the stage, and give it an instance name of `tiger_mc`.

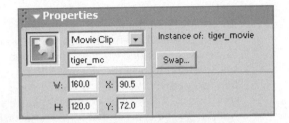

This is a very important step – if you forget to do this then you will not be able to control your movie using ActionScript.

10. Use the Align window, with the `To Stage` button selected, to align it to the center of the stage.

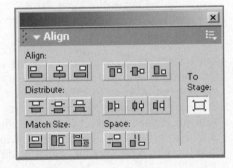

11. If you save your movie and test it, the tiger video should play.

Controlling the video

We don't have much control over our video: it just plays, and we can't stop or go back to the start. We've already seen how to use _prevFrame and _nextFrame actions, so we're going to wire these up to some buttons to allow users to stop, and move through the video clip how they want. We'll create the following buttons:

- Play the video.
- Stop the video.
- Go to the beginning of the video.
- Jump to the previous frame.
- Jump to the next frame.

We could create these ourselves, but we've already gone over all the concepts involved, so let's take it easy and make use of Flash's **common libraries.**

1. Go to Window > Common Libraries > Buttons. Here, you'll see a veritable smorgasbord of buttons. We want the Circle Buttons, so double-click on this folder to open it. With the buttons layer selected, drag a copy of the play button in this folder onto the stage below the tiger video.

2. Double-click to edit the button in place. When Macromedia built this button, they followed good practice and put separate items on three separate layers – one for the text, one for the triangle and one for the circle. We don't want to have any text on our final buttons – let's face it everybody knows what a Play button looks like. So we can lose the text layer, select it and then delete it by hitting the trashcan icon just below the layers.

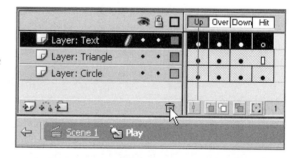

3. Our hit area was originally designed to cover the text we've just deleted, so we now need to edit this. Select the Hit state keyframe in the Circle layer and go to Insert > Clear Keyframe to remove the old Hit state. Having a clear keyframe here will also mean that this state inherits the same content as the Down state, which luckily is a

nice little circle just the size we need for
our Hit state – perfect!

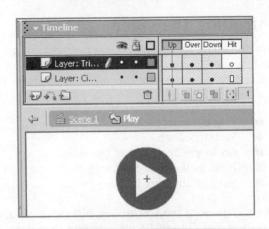

4. Repeat steps 1-3 with the stop, step
ahead, step back, and rewind buttons in
the Circle Buttons folder (note that the
top layer of the step back button is not
called text, but still contains the text and
needs deleting). Select all five buttons;
select the To Stage button if it's not
already selected, and use the Distribute
horizontal center and Align bottom
edge buttons to line them up as shown:

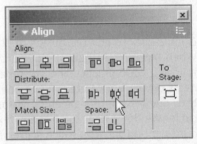

5. We are now going to add some script to
these buttons. Select the first frame of the
Scripts layer, and click F9 to bring up the
Actions window. In Expert mode, add the
following code:

```
tiger_mc.stop();
```

This uses the name of the instance on the
stage, tiger_mc and tells it to stop, so that
when the movie loads it will not play until
the user starts it.

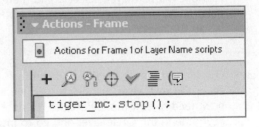

6. Now select the Play button and enter the following:

    ```
    on (release){
          tiger_mc.play();
    }
    ```

    Again, we're using the instance name `tiger_mc` – this time to tell the clip to start playing.

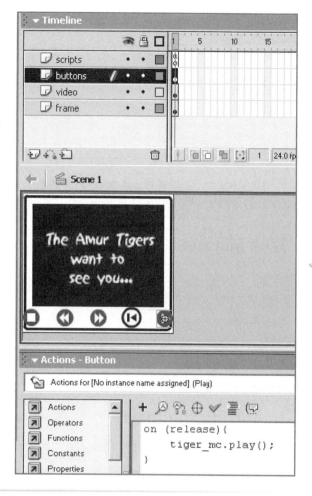

7. Click on the `step ahead` button and enter:

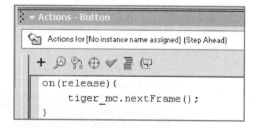

8. Click on the `stop` button and enter:

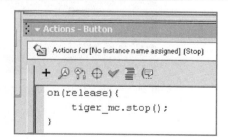

135

9.   Click on the `step back` button and enter:

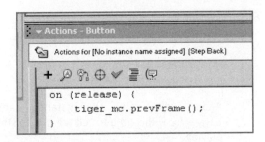

```
on (release) {
    tiger_mc.prevFrame();
}
```

10. The last button to put code on is the
     `rewind` button. This time, this is referring to
     the instance name, and telling the play head
     to go to and stop at frame number 1 – the
     start of the movie.

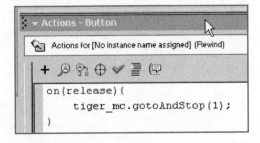

```
on(release){
    tiger_mc.gotoAndStop(1);
}
```

11. Save your file and test it. Make sure all the
     buttons work.

Importing the movie

So now you have your tiger video working quite nicely, it's time to bring it into your website.

1.   Open `animal_content.fla`, and move to
     the tiger frame — this is frame 6 of the `con-`
     `tent` layer. Select the image of the tiger
     and convert it to a movie clip called `video`.
     Double-click on the `video` movie clip to
     edit it in place.

SUMATRAN TIGER

The Sumatran is the smallest of the tiger
species. It is known for its reddish orange
hide with narrow black, gray or brown
stripes. Tigers have muscular front legs
with large paws armed with sharp claws.
They have strong back legs which are used
for pouncing on their prey. Males can grow
to a length of about 8 feet, while females
grow up to 7 feet. They vary in weight

video

‹ previous   return to full list   next ›

2. Rename the default layer content, and then add three more layers: Scripts, invisBtn, and text. Select frame 2 in all four layers and insert a blank keyframe. Place a stop() action in the scripts layer in frames 1 and 2.

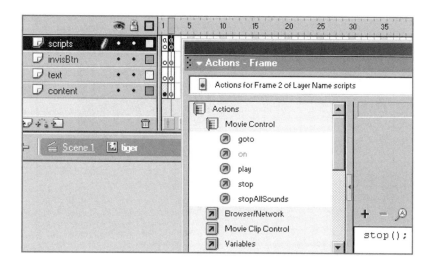

3. In frame 2 of the content layer, draw a rectangle with a solid fill, and use the Property inspector to make it 182x162 in size. Convert this rectangle into a movie clip and call it tiger_movie_place. Make sure the registration point is at the top left, as usual – if it's not, then the location we're about to set will be wrong.

4. Position this movie clip at (-99, -80), and give it an instance name of tigerMovie. As you might have guessed, this movie clip will function as a placeholder for us to load our video clip into.

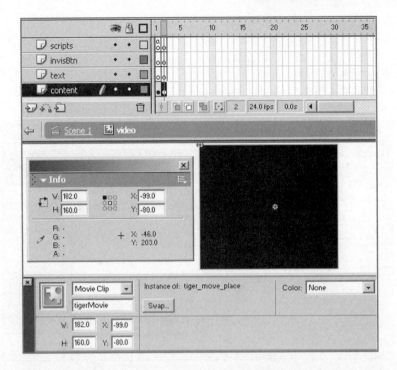

5. In frame 1 of the text layer, use size 16 Arial and write video on the stage. Position this at (122, 55), which should position it at the bottom right-hand corner of the tiger picture. In frame 2 of the same layer, write picture on the stage in the same font and size, and position this at (85, 59).

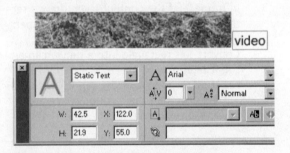

6. Drag an instance of the invs_btn that we created last session into both keyframes on the invisBtn layer. Position the buttons, and then re-size them with the Free Transform tool, so that they cover the words on the text layer.

7. Select the invisible button in the first keyframe (which should cover the video text nicely), and open the Actions window. Add a goto action, check the gotoAndStop radio button, and change the number in the Frame: box from 1 to 2.

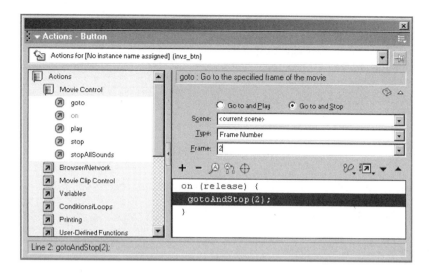

8. Select the button in the second keyframe, and add another goto action. Check the gotoAndStop radio button again, but leave the Frame: number as 1. When you've done this, save your movie and test it to check that the buttons work.

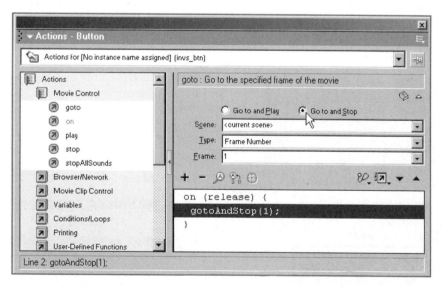

9. We are now going to use one line of ActionScript to tell Flash to load tiger_video into the tigerMovie place-

holder we've just created. Select the keyframe in frame 2 of the scripts layer. This should say `stop();` at the moment. Enter the line of code shown into it before the stop action. In English, this line of code says, *"Flash player, load tiger_video.swf, and put it into the placeholder called tigerMovie"*.

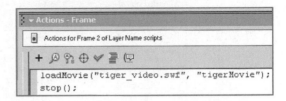

If you have NOT saved your `tiger_video.swf` *in the SAME folder as the* `animal_content.fla`, *then you will need to add the full path to that. For example, if it were in another folder, your path would be* `content/tiger_video.swf`. *For now, however, I'd encourage you to save everything in the same folder.*

10. Save your file and test it. Again, for this to work you will need to have your `tiger_video.swf`, in the same folder as `animal_content.swf`.

When you test your movie, you should see the picture of a tiger, and when you push the video button it should swap to the movie, with the buttons we built at the start of the session.

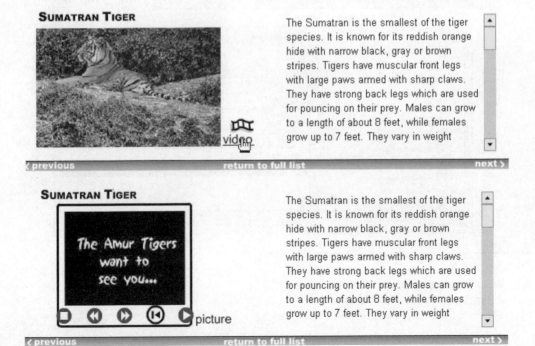

In this session, we have used ActionScript to load and control our video clip. In the next session, we'll learn even more about ActionScript as we use it to add a scrolling gallery to our website.

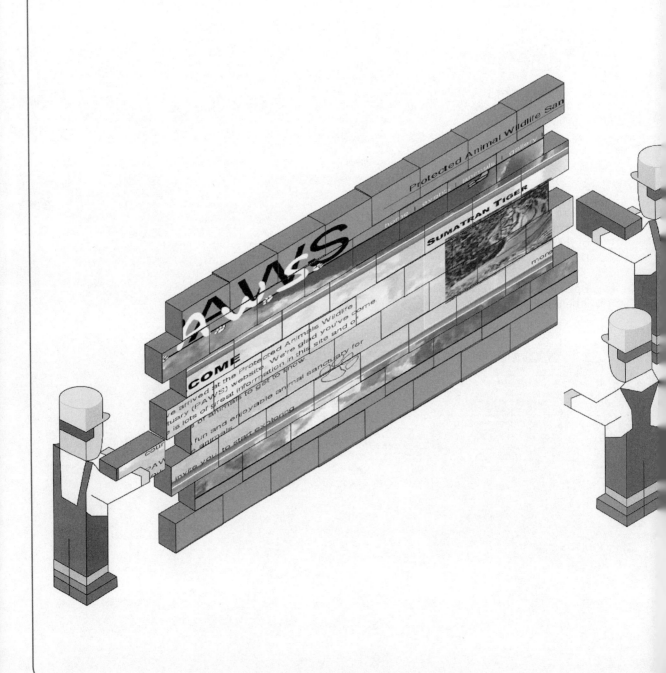

ActionScript Movement

In this session, we're going to create a gallery, with two buttons to scroll the images in the gallery to the left or right. This is going to involve a little ActionScript, but it is ActionScript that you can take away and reuse.

ActionScript is what makes Flash interactive. It can look quite foreign, if you don't have any programming experience, but if you take it a little bit at a time, it's not hard to learn.

First of all let's make sure you've got your Actions panel set to **Expert Mode**, which doesn't mean you're an expert already—but simply allows you to type directly into the panel, rather than use all those multiple choice options. You change this by twirling the small triangle in the upper right of the Actions panel. It will probably be set to **Normal Mode**, but check Expert Mode instead. Do this before proceeding, because Normal Mode will sometimes gobble up hand-written code!

Open gallery_content.fla, which we'll base this project on, and click on the frame with the little **a** in it, (for actions). Take a look at the code in the Actions window.

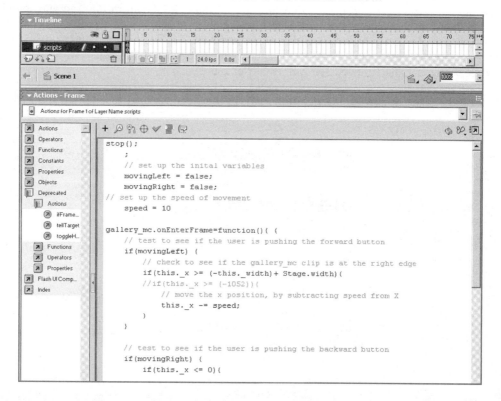

We'll be going through this step by step as the session proceeds, but I wanted to point a few things out at this stage. ActionScript is basically a series of instructions to the Flash Player, written in a very orderly way. It's a bit fussy and doesn't tolerate errors, so you need to watch your spelling and punctuation closely. If you type neatly or are good at cutting and pasting (!) you already move to the front of the class.

Punctuation is critical in making code function { and } define actions that the Flash player will perform, and just like in HTML, you need to make sure you have a closing } if you have an opening {, and a closing " if you have an opening ". Leaving them out will cause an error window to pop up when you test your movie.

You probably encountered **variables** in high school and may not have fond memories. But they're just named containers whose values may change. Look at these two statements:

```
Myglass="milk"
Myglass="water"
```

`Myglass` is a variable and the liquids named are its changing value. Variables themselves are never in quotes.

Functions do their job, they tell Flash what to do and are followed by braces, {}, with code sandwiched in between the braces. **Conditionals** are `if` statements that control what gets done. They start with an `if` and have a set of parentheses holding the statement to question.

```
if(the glass is empty){fill the glass!}
```

These are only the most basic tips and pointers, but there are lots of resources out there to help you get to grips with ActionScript. You could try downloading tutorials or FLAs from the web and spend some time going over the code is a great way to get comfortable using code. Check out the friends of ED beginners' guides to ActionScript: Foundation ActionScript for Flash MX (ISBN 190345073X), or ActionScript Zero to Hero (ISBN 190434119). Finally, the ActionScript Reference within Flash itself is another great way to familiarize yourself with what's possible.

Just click on the small book with the question mark in the Actions panel to open up the ActionScript Reference.

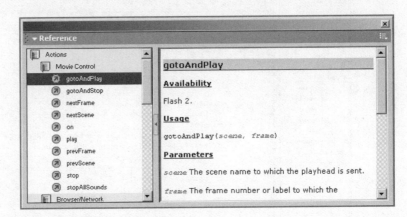

Now it's time to get this gallery moving.

1. Create a new Flash movie, and use Modify > Document to make the movie 640x216, so that it fits into the white area in the middle of our stage in the main paws file. Set the Frame Rate to 24 fps as usual, and save it as gallery_content.fla. Take a look at the screenshot to see what we will create:

    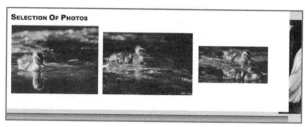

    ■ The white area is the stage.

    ■ The gray stripe at the bottom is our navigation (based on the one we used in Session nine).

    ■ The long group of eight pictures from around the park runs from left to right

2. Create five new layers, and then name your layers (top to bottom): scripts, title, navigation, whiteEdge, backing and content.

3. On the backing layer, create a keyframe in the second frame, and draw a strokeless black rectangle. Use the Property inspector to make it 640x216 in size. Set the location to X: 0, Y: 0 so that it covers the stage (we'll use this when this Flash file is imported into the main movie).

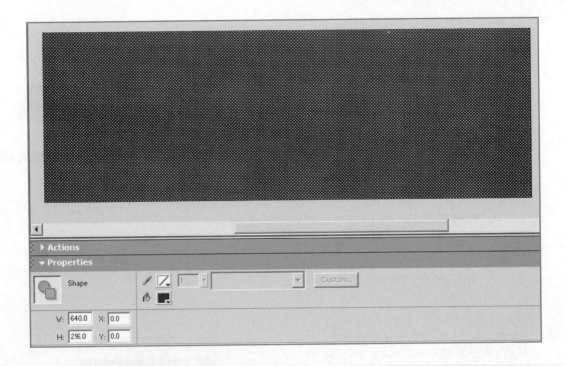

4. With frame 1 of the content layer selected, create a movie clip and call it gallery. Import the images found in the gallery folder on the CD, and place them on the stage in any order, left to right. To keep your Library compact, create a folder called photos in the Library, and move them into that.

5. Select all of the images, and bring up the Align panel. Make sure the To Stage button is selected, and choose Align vertical center. Then use the Distribute horizontal center option to space them out neatly.

6.   Select all of the images, and select Modify > Group to **group** the images so that we can move them around as one unit. Move the group so that it lines up with the registration point at 0,0.

7.   Return to the main timeline, and give the movie clip an instance name of gallery_mc and place it at (0, 9).

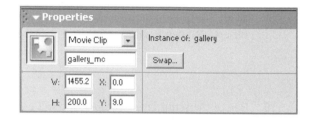

8.   We now have to create our navigation bar: Open animal_content.fla, and drag base_nav from the animal content library to your gallery content library. Close the animal content movie.

9.   Drag an instance of `base_nav` into the navigation layer, and place it at the bottom of the stage. Give it an instance name of `base_mc`. We don't need the bar to animate into place, so we'll modify this movie clip now. Double-click to edit in place. Select frames 1-4 on all layers, (making sure no layers are locked) and remove these frames. (Insert>Remove Frames or SHIFT + F5).

10.   Delete the script layer. All our code will be in that first frame of our main movie. Finally, change the one-frame green tween in the base layer back to None.

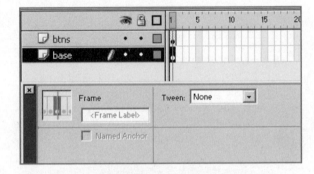

11.   We don't need the `return to full list` button here, so simply select it and hit DELETE to remove it. Double-click on the *previous* button to edit in place, delete the Paws layer. Now, with the Over frame selected, change the text on the button from `previous` to `backward`.

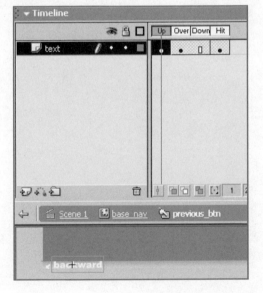

12. Now select the `Over` state keyframe too, again change the text to backward, but this time you need to make the font black.

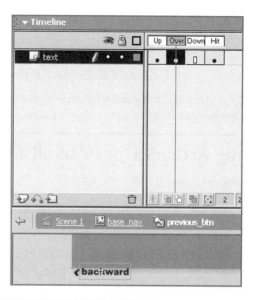

13. Repeat this with the next button, but this time change the text from `next` to `for-ward`, remember to change the text for the `Over` state, and remove the `Paws` layer for this button too. Give the forward button an instance name of `moveleft_btn`, and the backward button an instance name of `moveright_btn`.

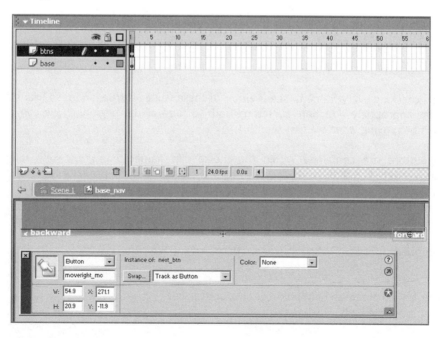

Button instance names are a new feature introduced in Flash MX.

By reusing this navigation bar, we've not only saved ourselves some time, but we've also kept things consistent across the site so that the user can easily navigate around.

Using ActionScript to scroll the gallery

Now we'll set up some ActionScript for the two buttons to tell `gallery_mc` to move either left or right. We want to have `gallery_mc` moving as long as the user is pressing a button, and stop when that button is released. We know that Flash can tell us when someone presses a button and we can script actions to reflect that.

What we're going to do here is a little more complex: we're going to tell Flash to detect when someone clicks on a button, and then set a **flag**, a kind of coded 'on' or 'off' signal, that indicates they've done this. We can then take that flag value, and have some action repeat continuously as long as it's on, and stop when the flag is switched off. There's no flag to actually see; it's just a term to indicate how this variable or value, that can be true or false, will function.

Because of the new features of MX, we can put all our code for this gallery movie into one frame on the `scripts` layer on the main timeline. So click on that frame and let's start coding.

Our variables, or code flags, will be called `movingLeft` for the `moveleft_btn` button, and `movingRight` for the `moveright_btn` button. Although we referred to switching them on and off, in fact we do the same by referring to these flag variable values as `true` or `false` – `true` is on and `false` is off.

Enter this code into frame 1 of the `scripts` layer of our main timeline.

```
movingLeft = false;
    movingRight = false;
```

Flash will be checking every frame to see if either of these values is true, and if so, will start moving our gallery in the appropriate direction. By setting both to false at the beginning, we can ensure that the gallery won't be moving when we first see it!

Since our buttons are contained within the movie clip named `base_mc`, we'll refer to them as `base_mc.moveleft_btn` and `base_mc.moveright_btn`. Without the prefix of `base_mc`, Flash couldn't find them, since the buttons are inside the movie clip `base_mc`.

Here's the code for our two buttons. Add this below the flag statements we just typed:

```
base_mc.moveright_btn.onPress=function(){
    movingRight = true;
}
base_mc.moveright_btn.onRelease=function(){
    movingRight = false;
```

```
    }

base_mc.moveleft_btn.onPress=function(){
    movingLeft = true;
}
base_mc.moveleft_btn.onRelease=function(){
    movingLeft = false;

    }
base_mc.moveleft_btn.onReleaseOutside=base_mc.moveleft_btn.onRelease;
base_mc.moveright_btn.onReleaseOutside=base_mc.moveright_btn.onRelease;
```

We've added those two long lines at the bottom to make sure our button sends the message, even if the user moves their mouse off the button before releasing the mouse. The code sets the same action for onReleaseOutside as for onRelease for each button.

That takes care of our buttons. But if you tested it now the gallery still wouldn't move. Save your file. We're going to get things moving.

We need to tell Flash what to do when movingLeft or movingRight become true. If we use an onEnterFrame command, it will check this every time it enters a new frame on the timeline, which we've set to 24 times a second. Immediately after the last code, enter:

```
gallery_mc.onEnterFrame=function(){
    if(movingLeft) {
            this._x -= 10;
        }

    if(movingRight) {
            this._x += 10;
            }
    }
```

The first line of this code is addressing gallery_mc, and telling it that when it enters each frame, onEnterFrame, it must do this function(){

Then, using an **if** statement, we ask it to check "is movingLeft set to true?" This is called a **conditional**, meaning that we are telling Flash to follow the next instruction if a specific condition is met.

```
    if(movingLeft==true)
```

(Note the double == sign for testing equality in ActionScript). Our first version however, means exactly the same thing and is easier to type!

```
    if(movingLeft)
```

Then we tell the Flash player, if it is set to true, move this movie clip (gallery_mc) 10 pixels to the left, or, in code, this._x- =10. Notice the necessary braces { } around the action.

> *Always make sure if you have one brace, that the code ends with another closing brace, or the code will produce an error window when you test it.*

'this._x' refers to the `gallery_mc`'s _x position.

x, as you know, is where this clip is located horizontally on the stage. The `gallery_mc` had an _x position of 0 at the outset.

`this.x-=10` is shorthand for `this._x=this._x-10`, and likewise `this._x+ = 10` is shorthand for `this._x = this._x +10`.

You can write them either way, but the way I've coded it is just more compact.

So if the `gallery_mc` is currently at X position 0, and we subtract 10 from this, the `gallery_mc` is moved to X position -10, and continues to be moved to 10 pixels less in its X position on each frame, as long as the button is held down. There's no problem in setting the _x value to a negative number, though you do sometimes need to surround that negative value with brackets.(-10)

If you save and test the movie now, it should work except - it still needs code to keep it from running away off screen, and this code will need to set boundaries so the edges never show.

For the left edge it's easy to tell it where to stop... as long as _x is less than 0, it can keep moving to the right, because the left edge hasn't appeared on the stage yet. Think about it. If _x was greater than 0 and it was moving to the right, we'd see the left edge of the movie clip - ugly!

For the right edge we need more code.

Flash has access to a lot of information about movie clips – just open the ActionScript dictionary and look under Properties to see all the properties that can be controlled. It also has access to information about other objects, like the stage. `Stage.width` will tell us the width of the stage, 640 pixels. (We know the size already because that's the size of our movie, but it's nice that Flash knows it too!)

Our movie clip width we can get from the Property Inspector. Mine says 1692 pixels, your mileage may vary! So imagine this : if we moved this movie clip all the way over to the left so its right edge was butted against stage left, the X value for `gallery_mc` would be –1692 or (`-this._width`), wouldn't it? (I'm saying negative `this._width`, with `this` referring to `gallery_mc`). Because, remember the edge of the stage is 0, and now our X position is the full length of our movie clip in negative.

But we need to set our limits so the right side of the movie clip just covers the stage, not butts against the right edge. If we add the width of the stage to our big negative number, we should have the boundary edge we need, a negative number of only (–1692) + 640 = (-1052).

That's then as far to the left as the movie clip can be moved without its right edge appearing, negative 1052. We can write this numerically or abstractly.

Numerically the code would be: `if(this._x >= (-1052)){`

Or abstractly it would be: `if(this._x >= (-this._width)+ Stage.width){`

Both will work, but the abstract version is easier to adapt to other projects, and besides, your movie clip may not be the same length as mine.

Save your file, and test it. It should scroll when you press down the appropriate buttons, but stop on each side when it's reached its defined boundaries.

Another way to work out the X value that you need the gallery to scroll to, is to simply select the gallery movie clip on the main timeline and move it to the left using the Arrow tool, until you the right edge of the clip is on the stage, make a note of the x value shown in the Property inspector, such as 992, and then insert the following code:

`if(this._x >= (-992)){`

One more thing. Let's try putting the amount to move the clip each frame inside a variable named `speed`, so you can easily change the value and it will affect both directions.

At the top of your code, just below `stop();` add `speed = 10`. Now go into the two sections where it says `_x - =10` and `_x + =10`, and change them to `_x - = speed` and `_x + = speed`.

Check that your entire script for this frame looks like the code below. The // lines are comments I've added.

> *Flash allows you to put* **comments** *into your ActionScript to help you remember what different bits of code are there for when you come back to your Flash site after six months and can't remember anything. When Flash runs the ActionScript, it will ignore comments completely, so you can put whatever you want in them. You add a comment by putting // before whatever you want to say, as long as it stays on one line.*

```
stop();
    ;
    // set up the inital variables
    movingLeft = false;
    movingRight = false;
// set up the speed of movement
    speed = 10

gallery_mc.onEnterFrame=function(){ {
    // test to see if the user is pushing the forward button
    if(movingLeft) {
        // check to see if the gallery_mc clip is at the right edge
        //if(this._x >= (-this._width)+ Stage.width){
        if(this._x >= (-1052)){
            // move the x position, by subtracting speed from X
            this._x -= speed;
```

```
                    }
            }

            // test to see if the user is pushing the backward button
            if(movingRight) {
                    if(this._x <= 0){

                            // move the x position by adding speed to X
                            this._x += speed;
                    }
            }

}}
stop();
base_mc.moveright_btn.onPress=function(){
      movingRight = true;
}

base_mc.moveright_btn.onRelease=function(){
      movingRight = false;
}

base_mc.moveleft_btn.onPress=function(){
      movingLeft = true;
}

base_mc.moveleft_btn.onRelease=function(){
      movingLeft = false;

}
base_mc.moveleft_btn.onReleaseOutside= base_mc.moveleft_btn.onRelease;
base_mc.moveright_btn.onReleaseOutside= base_mc.moveright_btn.onRelease;
```

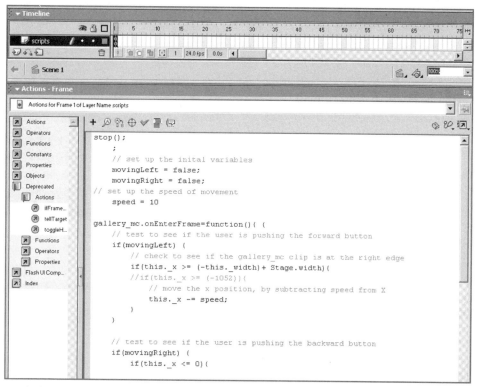

```
stop();
    ;
    // set up the inital variables
    movingLeft = false;
    movingRight = false;
// set up the speed of movement
    speed = 10

gallery_mc.onEnterFrame=function(){ {
    // test to see if the user is pushing the forward button
    if(movingLeft) {
        // check to see if the gallery_mc clip is at the right edge
        if(this._x >= (-this._width)+ Stage.width){
        //if(this._x >= (-1052)){
            // move the x position, by subtracting speed from X
            this._x -= speed;
        }
    }

    // test to see if the user is pushing the backward button
    if(movingRight) {
        if(this._x <= 0){
```

Save your Flash movie and test it. You can now vary the amount in the variable speed to see how it looks scrolling faster and slower. If the scrolling doesn't work, check the following four most common errors in ActionScript:

- Does your gallery movie clip have the correct instance name? It should be `gallery_mc`.

- Do your buttons have the correct instance names? They should be `moveleft_btn` and `moveright_btn`. Does the navigation bar have an instance name of `base_mc`?

- Is your punctuation correct and complete?

- Have you spelled `movingRight`/`movingLeft` correctly with capitals in the right places? Code is usually case sensitive.

- Is the code in the frame, where it should be, or on the movie clip?

Adding a border

Before we finish, we're going to add an extra touch. We're going to cut out the edge of the taller images, and make sure that they're only visible in the center of the stage.

1. On the `title` layer, add the title
    `Selection of Photos` in size 22 _sans.

2. On the `whiteEdge` layer, draw a white rec-
    tangle, with no stroke, just slightly larger
    than the stage and position it at (-5,-5).
    Make sure it covers the stage. As long as
    your layers are in the right order, you'll be
    able to see your title text, but nothing else.

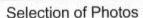

3. In the same layer, draw a green rectangle
    onto the white one, in the area you want to
    see the images.

4. Select the green rectangle, and delete it.
    This will leave a white border that will frame
    our photos nicely. You may need to adjust
    this a bit until it suits you. The idea is to
    make a nice picture frame that your gallery

images will appear in.

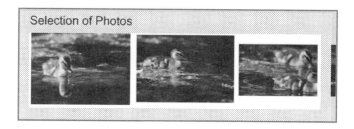

5 Save the file, and pat yourself on the back. It's been a heavy session with that scripting, but you've done really well.

Further steps

This session has probably been the hardest one we've gone through yet, but hopefully you can see the rewards for yourselves. You've just created a scrolling photo gallery in Flash. If you've got some images of your own that you'd like to present in a gallery, then now's the time to go and make a nice little Flash movie of them...

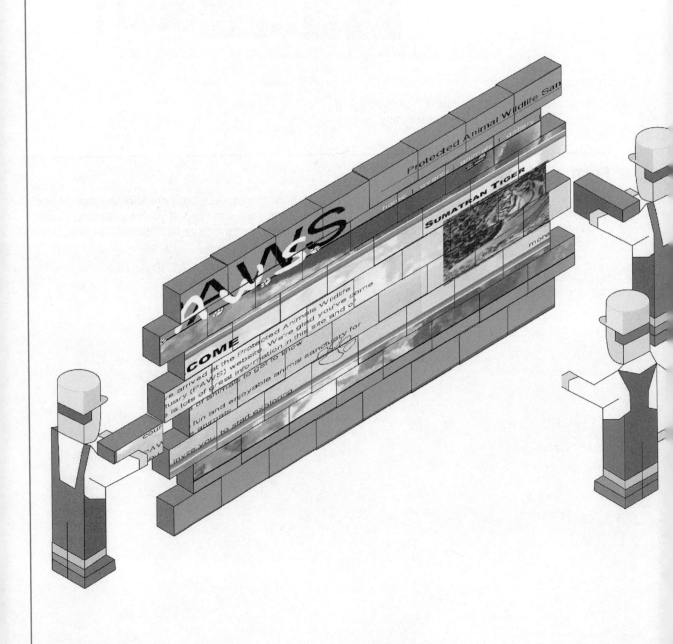

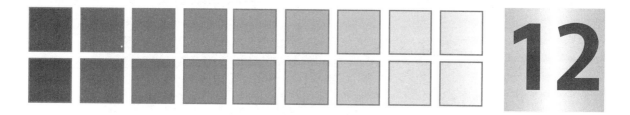

Interactive Content

We've built the content for the event, animal and gallery sections, so we've just two more to complete: the about us and contact pages.

1. Create a new Flash movie, and set it to the usual settings of 640x216 and 24fps. Save it as about_content.fla. Take a look at the screenshot to see what we're going to create: a simple page with some text.

2. Add three layers, and name them, top to bottom: scripts, buttons, content and backing.

3. In the backing layer, create a black rectangle without a stroke, and use the Property inspector to make it 640x216. Position it at (0,0) so that it covers the stage.

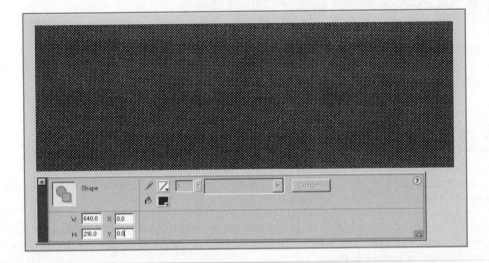

4. Bring up the Color Mixer window, as we're going to add a gradient fill to our rectangle. Set the fill in the drop-down box to `Linear`. Select the house-shaped point to the right, and set it to 0% alpha using the slider just above the bar. Click on the other "house," drag it in a little to the right, turn it white, and give it an alpha value of 62%.

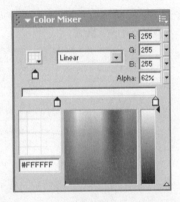

5. This gradient is currently white on white, so at the moment you won't see any effect. If you want to see the effect now, then you could make the grid visible, (View > Grid > Show Grid) or even temporarily change the background color to something bright. Just make sure you change the background color back to white again before publishing! When you're finished, lock the `backing` layer to make sure you don't move it by accident when working on other layers.

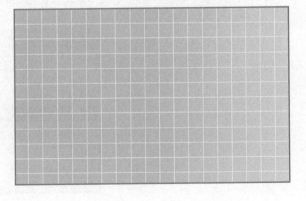

6. On the `content` layer, select the Text tool, and choose size 12 `Arial` font from the Property inspector. Set it to `Static Text`.

Since this is our basic information about the site, we don't expect it to change and don't need to make it dynamic. Draw a text box on the left-hand side of the stage, with enough room above it for a title. Type this text into the box:

```
PAWS is an animal park that aims
to protect rare breeds and allows
them to enjoy as natural a
habitat as possible.
Formed in 1990, and opened to
the public in 1995, PAWS welcomes
thousands of visitors annually.

PAWS offers a number of services:
    Packages tailored to schools
    and young people.
    Unique guided tours.
    Information and pictures of
    your favorite animals online.

For more details, please contact
us.
```

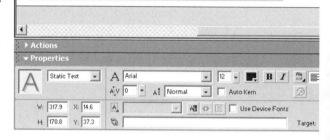

7. For a title, add About Paws in size 20 Arial Black, and use the Align panel to line it up with the left-hand side PAWS text. On the right hand side, add Visit Us in another static box with the same font settings as the title. Use the Align vertical center button to line the two up vertically.

About PAWS

PAWS is an animal park that aims to protect rare breeds and allows them to enjoy as natural a habitat as possible. Formed in 1990, and opened to the public in 1995, PAWS welcomes thousands of visitors annually.

PAWS offers a number of services:
    Packages tailored to schools and young people.
    Unique guided tours.
    Information and pictures of your favorite animals online.

For more details, please contact us.

Visit Us

You do not need to click the To Stage button in the Align panel as you are aligning the text boxes to each other, rather than to the stage.

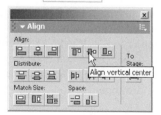

Next, we need to add two links, one for email, and the other for navigation. We now need to make an invisible button to cover the words contact us in the main text. We'll do this in exactly the same we did in Session 9.

8. Click on the buttons layer and make a rectangle that covers the words contact us. Convert this to a graphic symbol called generic_rectangle and then while still selected convert to a button called invs_btn. Double click this button to edit it in place and drag the keyframe from the Up state to the Hit state. This creates an invisible button the size of the rectangle in the Hit state.

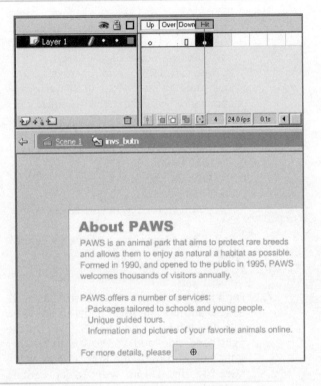

9. So now you have your invisible button, return to the main timeline and give it an instance name of contact. You may be wondering why we need to create a button here, as the words contact us are not obviously a link, the idea is that if someone does try to click there, then they won't be disappointed, as it will link to our email address. On the actual contact page, which we'll work on next, the email link will be more prominent.

10. Drag an instance of the invisible button out of the Library and place it over the Visit Us text too. (Use the Free Transform tool to

scale it). Give that button an instance name of `visit`. Finally, we need to add the script to make these buttons work. Click on the layer named `scripts`. Add these scripts to the Actions panel:

```
visit.onPress=function(){
_root.gotoAndStop("contact");}

contact.onPress=function(){
getURL("mailto:bigcat@paws.net?subject=
➥a question")}

Stop()
```

Save your file and test it. When you click on the email link, the subject line is already filled out for you.

About PAWS

PAWS is an animal park that aims to protect rare breeds and allows them to enjoy as natural a habitat as possible. Formed in 1990, and opened to the public in 1995, PAWS welcomes thousands of visitors annually.

PAWS offers a number of services:
Packages tailored to schools and young people.
Unique guided tours.
Information and pictures of your favorite animals online.

For more details, please contact us.

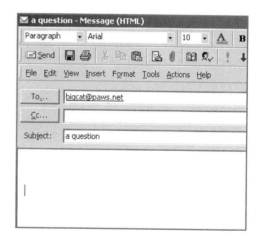

Contact page

Our Contact page will again be a simple one-page affair. We're going to create a basic map so that people know where we are, how to get there, and how to contact us. We'll add a little animation of a car to make the page more fun.

CONTACT PAWS

Physical Address:
Corner of Leigh Rd and River Rd
Orewa
New Zealand

Postal Address:
P.O Box 453
Orewa
New Zealand

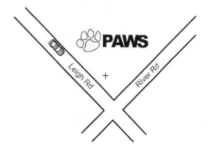

1. Create a new Flash document, and give it the usual settings of our site: 640x216 and 24fps. Save it as `contact_content.fla`. Create two new layers, and name your layers (from top to bottom): `scripts`, `map`, and `content`. On the `content` layer, select the Text tool, and choose the usual size 12 `_Sans` from the Property inspector. Add an address on the left-hand side of the page, as pictured. In another text box, add `Contact PAWS` in size 20 bold `Arial` as a title, and line it up with the address box.

Let's make an email link for this page, just as we have did for the `about us` page: Drag the invisible button from the `about_content` library to the `contact_content` library. Now drag an instance of this button over the `Contact PAWS` text in the `content` layer, and resize it using the Free Transform tool. You can give this button an instance name of `contact` just as we did before; as ultimately our two contact buttons will be in separate movie clips, so it doesn't matter that they have the same name. Now place the following ActionScript in the `scripts` frame:

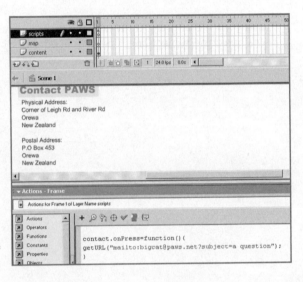

```
contact.onPress=function(){
getURL("mailto:bigcat@paws.net?subject=
➥a question");
}
stop();
```

2. Insert a new movie clip symbol and call it `map`. For our map, we want a simple crossroads set up at a 45-degree angle. Using the Line tool set to 2.25 pixels, draw a solid black stroke about 500 pixels wide. Draw a second parallel line spaced about 30 pixels lower. Use the Info panel to check your Y mouse position to measure 30 pixels.

3. Select the Text tool, and position a text box towards the left-hand side of the screen, between the two lines. Type in `Leigh Road`, at size 20 `Arial`. Select the two lines and the

text box and group them so we can turn them together to our desired angle, by going to Modify>Group. Using the Free Transform tool, rotate the group 45 degrees.

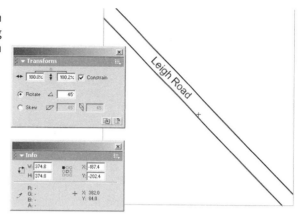

Copy the group, and then paste it again in the same layer. Now rotate this second road —45 degrees, so that it forms a cross pattern with the other road. Move this second road to the left and downward until you're satisfied with the position. Finally, break both groups apart, change the name of the second road to River Road and reposition this text box to suit the design. Use the Eraser to delete the lines at the center of the crossroads and to neaten up the overall design; you should now have an intersection with two named streets.

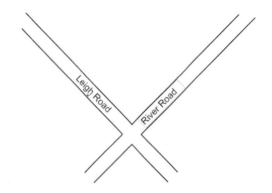

4. Select File > Open as Library, and open your Paws.fla file (or Paws02.fla from the CD). Drag an instance of logo_complete symbol onto your stage, and close the Library. Set the size of the paw to about 30% using the Transform panel, and rotate the logo roughly –15 degrees.

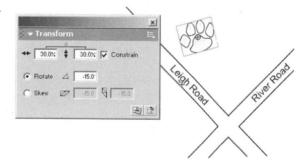

5. Above it, enter the title text PAWS, I used size 70 Arial Black font with the character spacing set to –10 (using the slider underneath the font, as shown). This logo will identify the location of PAWS on the map. Lock this layer.

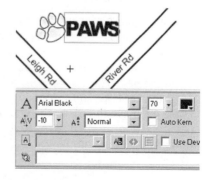

165

6.   Now add a new layer in the map movie clip called `car` and then click the `Add Motion Guide` icon to add a guide layer for the car, just as we did in Session 2.

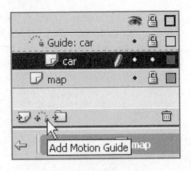

7.   Select the `car` layer, and now either draw a car or import the image, `car_01.gif` from the CD. If you are drawing your own car, remember that it'll be quite small so it doesn't need to be too detailed, but you do need to draw the car bigger than the map and then scale it down. Once you're done, convert your car into a graphic symbol called `car`. Make sure the registration point is the front center of the car.

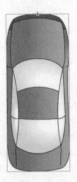

8.   Use the Pencil tool to draw a path for the car to follow on the `guide` layer. Set the line to ink, but if it wobbles too much go to Modify>Smooth to make it a smoother path. The path should start from out of screen top, down Leigh Rd, and then turn in at PAWS.

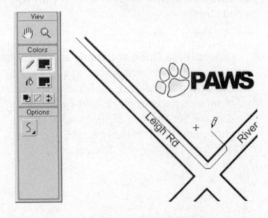

9.   Drag an instance of your `car` graphic into the `car` layer. Use the Free Transform tool to rotate the car roughly 135 degrees and then scale it down, so it's headed properly down the path. Place a keyframe in frame 40 of the car layer and the guide layer. At frame 40, move the car to the end of the line, and rotate it -45 degrees so it looks as though it's driving into PAWS.

10. Click on the car layer and choose `Motion Tween` from the `Tween:` drop-down in the Property inspector. Check `Orient to Path` and `Snap`. Set the easing to `50 Out`, so that the car slows slightly before it stops. Test your animation by scrubbing (moving mouse back and forward) through the timeline.

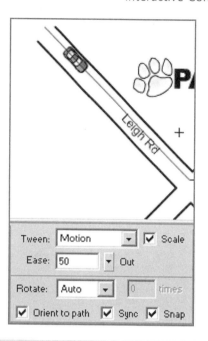

11. Click in frame 80 of the `map` layer so the map frames extend out farther in time. Because the map layer extends to frame 80, it will appear that every now and again a car comes in and drives to PAWS. I think this makes PAWS look popular. But if this gets on your nerves, add a simple `stop();` action to the last frame of the `map` layer and your animation will play just once. Save your file, and test it.

Further steps

This has been a long session, and – once you've had a rest - you probably want to run on and do the next session, where everything starts to come together. There's plenty of room for you to take what we've done further, though.

For example, you're probably not going to get a set of directions as easy as our "crossroads", so you could go back and experiment with some trickier maps. Our car is OK, but it's not that interesting, so you could replace it with a movie clip of an animal moving along, or something else to keep folks entertained. On the CD files, you'll notice that I've added a couple of different cars coming at our map from different directions.

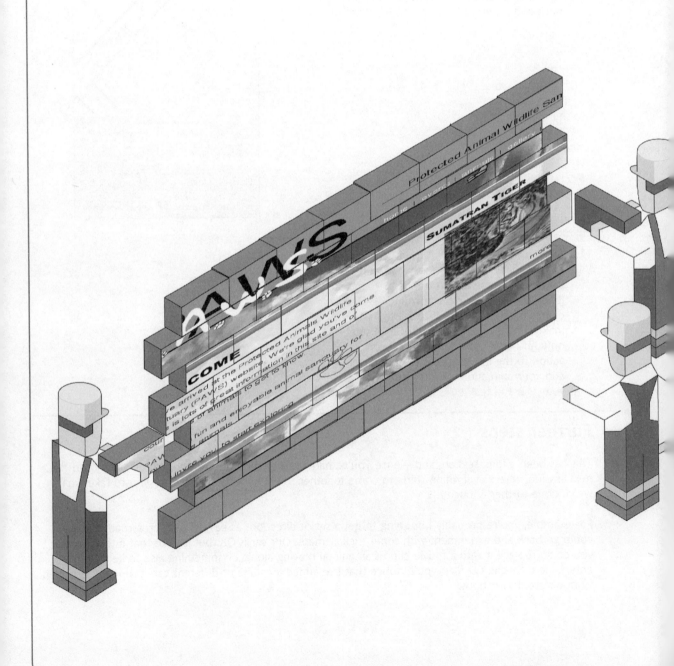

Loading Content

So far, we've created all our separate pages for the site. Now it's time to put all the jigsaw pieces together to create our site. In this session, we're going to set up the loading of these elements into the main PAWS site:

- the text for the events page
- the picture gallery (gallery_content.swf)
- the about page (about_content.swf)
- the contact page (contact_content.swf)
- the page displaying random animals (smalls.swf)
- the animal details page (animal_content.swf)
- the sound file (audio.fla)

Before we get to the loading in, we'll create the file that displays our random animals (smalls.swf).

Random pictures

In the completed PAWS site, there will be a small picture of an animal on the home page. Each time you visit the site, there's a chance you'll see a different picture, as the image will be loaded randomly. Some of these animals will have a more link, allowing the user to go straight to the animal's specific content page.

1. Open a new Flash movie. Give it a size of 200 x 200, our usual 24 fps setting, and save it as smalls.fla.

2. Rename the default layer images. Import the nine images found in the small_image folder (File > Import) by choosing the lowest numbered picture in the sequence. Flash will detect that the images are part of a numbered sequence and ask whether you want to import all the files in the sequence: say Yes, and they will come in as separate keyframes.

3. Select each picture in turn, and use the
    Property inspector to position it at (0,0).
    Lock the images layer so that we can't
    move the pictures away from their (0,0)
    positioning. Add three new layers, and call
    them: scripts, btns, and text.

4. In the btns layer, we need to create an
    invisible button the size of the pictures.
    Select the first frame of the btns layer, and
    draw a strokeless black rectangle that covers
    the tiger exactly, and convert this to a but-
    ton called invs_btn. Convert it to an invisi-
    ble button by dragging the Up keyframe
    across to the Hit frame, as we have been
    doing in previous examples. Now there will
    be a transparent blue rectangle over the
    images. Give this button an instance name
    of invs_btn.

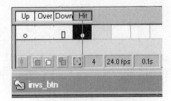

5. Select the first frame of the `text` layer and the Text tool. Use size 18 `Arial` to add the text "`more` ..." to the bottom right-hand corner of the picture, to let the user know that there's more information available for this animal. Make sure the button also covers this text or else they'll click on the word and nothing will happen.

6. Add keyframes to frames 1-9 of the `text` layer. Using the Text tool, choose size 20 `Arial`. For each picture, enter a title into the appropriate keyframe, and position it at (-25, -25). In order, these are: `Sumatran Tiger`, `Pink Cockatiel`, `Cockatiel`, `Giant Tortoise`, `Giraffe`, `Lion Cubs`, `African Lion`, `Ringtailed Lemur`, and `Spring Duckling`.

7. Add keyframes to each of the nine frames in the `btns` layer. Each picture should now have an invisible button in front of it with the instance name of `invs_btn`. However, since we don't have further information in the animal content section for the Pink Cockatiel, the Cockatiel, the Lion cubs, or the Spring Duckling, remove the invisible buttons for these four by clicking on the button in those keyframes and deleting it, and also delete the word "more..." in those frames. Your timeline should now look as shown.

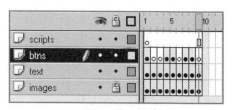

8. Select the first frame of the `scripts` layer, and add a `stop();` action to make sure that Flash doesn't run through our timeline before we want it to.

9. We want the random display of one picture when the movie clip is loaded, so we need to add a little code for that. On the first frame of our `smalls.fla scripts` layer, place this code.

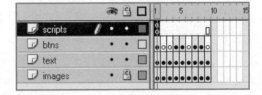

```
frameNum =
➡Math.Ceil(Math.random()*9);
gotoAndStop(frameNum);
```

> `Math.random` *gives us a number between 0 and 1. By multiplying it we get a value between 0 and 9.* `Math.ceil` *rounds any value* **up** *to the nearest integer, giving us a random value between 1 and 9 – which is the number of frames in our timeline. We then use* `gotoAndStop` *to stop at the random frame.*

Our invisible buttons are in the `smalls.fla` Flash file, which will be loaded into a movie clip in our main `paws.fla`, but the buttons will be controlling the content in another file entirely, going to a specific frame to display further information about a particular animal.

So how can we script buttons in one movie clip to control which frame to display in another? The content we want the buttons to display is contained in `animal_content.fla`, which will be loaded into `animal_content_mc`. The buttons need to send us to a particular frame label in `animal_content_mc`. Phew!

To deal with this, we need to store something in paws.swf that both files can get hold of. We're going to do this by telling Flash to store something on level 0 of paws.swf. Think of this as being like a specific shelf in the storeroom. So, in smalls.swf, we want to store where we want to go, and tell paws.swf to remember this. We then want to go to animal_content.swf, and ask paws.swf to give us the information we told it to remember for us.

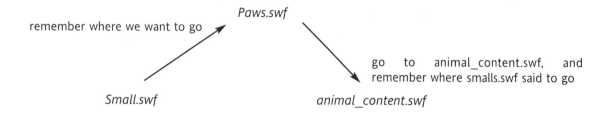

remember where we want to go → *Paws.swf*

go   to   animal_content.swf,   and
remember where smalls.swf said to go

Small.swf   *animal_content.swf*

10. In essence, then, what we're saying is: *Hey Flash player, on level 0 of paws.swf, store the word tiger in the animalTarget container... and then go to the animals frame label.* Select the invisible button over the tiger (not the frame with the button in it, the button itself), and enter the code shown in the screenshot:

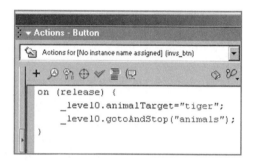

11. Add the same code to the other four invisible buttons, changing the name of the animal in the second line to `tortoise`, `giraffe`, `lion`, and `ringTail`, leaving the rest as it is. For example, the code for the next button should read:

```
on (release) {

_level0.animalTarget="tortoise";

_level0.gotoAndStop("animals");
}
```

On the `_root` level of our big site movie for PAWS we will add this code to the scripts:

```
// our invisible button
random_mc.invs_btn.onPress =
function() {
```

SUMATRAN TIGER

The Sumatran is the smallest of the tiger species. It is known for its reddish orange hide with narrow black, gray or brown stripes. Tigers have muscular front legs with large paws armed with sharp claws. They have strong back legs which are used for pouncing on their prey. Males can grow to a length of about 8 feet, while females grow up to 7 feet. They vary in weight

video

‹ previous   return to full list   next ›

12. Save your file, publish it, and test it, then test it again and again. Each time you've got a 1 in 9 chance of seeing the same picture and an 8 in 9 chance of a different animal picture.

> *Step forward, and you should be able to imagine many different uses for our random code. Think of a random quotes generator, for example, or a random picture from your collection of digital photos to display on the front of your web page. As long as each frame contains a different image or text, all you'd need to do to modify our random code is change the number of items from which the random number is to be chosen.*

Loading the files into the main movie

Dynamic text

1. Open Notepad or SimpleText. When we're creating text documents to load into a Flash document, we have to put each specific section of text inside & & symbols. To start the text we have to give it a name to refer to it in Flash, so our text will look like &name=text...&. Here, we're going to refer to our text as eventText, so start off by entering:

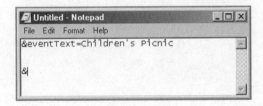

Note that we've got word wrap turned on here, otherwise everything would be on one line.

2. Even though this is a simple text file, Flash will add carriage returns for you, and observe your formatting. So you only need one carriage return to create a line between each paragraph. Between `Children's Picnic` and the closing `&`, add something like this:

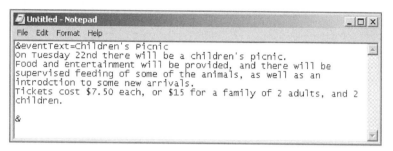

Notice there are no quotes used in this text file.

3. Save this as `text.txt` in the same directory as `paws.fla`. Open your PAWS file in Flash, and go to the `events` layer. Select the keyframe under the `events` label that we added the text field and title to earlier. Select the text field and scrollbar, and convert them to a movie clip called `eventText`. Give the movie clip an instance name of `eventText_mc`.

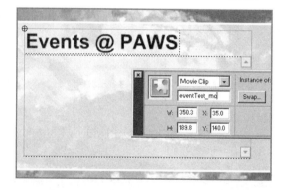

4. Double-click on the movie clip to edit it in place. Rename the default layer `content` and create a new layer called `scripts`. Create a blank keyframe in frame 2 of both layers. Select the keyframe in frame 1 and drag the content into frame 2, leaving a blank frame at frame 1. You'll see why in a minute.

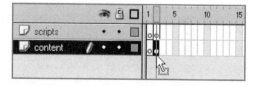

5. Add a `stop();` action to each of the two frames on the `scripts` layer. In frame 1 of the `content` layer, select the Text tool. Choose size 12 `Verdana`, and type `..Loading Events..` (in `Static Text`). Position this on the left of the stage, about halfway down.

6. Check the settings for the main text field in frame 2 of the `content` layer. The instance name should be `textScroll`. In the `Var:` box on the right of your Property inspector, enter the same name we set in our text file earlier – `eventText`.

7. Return to the main time line, and select the frame under the `event` label on the `scripts` layer. Open the Actions panel – you should find that it currently has a `stop();` action in it. We want the Flash player to load the text in the `text.txt` file to the `eventText` movie clip. To achieve this, add this line above the `stop();` action:

```
eventText_mc.loadVariables("text.
txt");
```

8. This will load your text, but because we're loading it in from an external file, it might take a moment or so to load. This sometimes means that Flash creates the text field and scrollbar for an empty text field, and then doesn't adjust the scrollbar when the contents arrive – leaving some of our text frustratingly inaccessible. To avoid this, we need to check that `text.txt` has loaded while our movie clip displays that `loading event details` text we placed on frame 1. We want to ask our movie clip `eventText_mc` whether it's received the data. If it has, then we want it to go and show the text (which will have loaded into frame 2) to the user. Enter this after the line we've just entered:

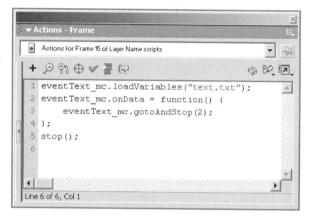

```
eventText_mc.onData = function()
{
    eventText_mc.gotoAndStop(2);
};
```

9. Save your file and test your movie, and you should see your events page with the text loaded in nicely. You probably won't see your `loading event details` text, as the text will load up pretty quickly on your local machine. Upload the files to a live server, though, and you will probably find things slow down a bit.

Loading the "contact", "about", and "gallery" SWFs

In order to bring in our other Flash files (these will be as SWFs – the files we create when we test our Flash movies, and not as FLAs), we're going to create an empty movie clip. This will act as a placeholder that we can load our SWFs into with a `loadmovie` ActionScript command.

1. Back on the main timeline, create a new movie clip, and call it `placeholder`. Don't add anything to this yet, but drag an instance of it from the Library into the keyframe under the `gallery` label in the `gallery` layer. (You may need to unlock the layer to do this.) Give it an instance name of `gallery_mc`, and (X,Y) values of (0, 131) – this should position it at exactly the top left-hand corner of the white band, as you can see from the screenshot.

2. We are now going to load our `gallery.swf` into our placeholder movie clip (which we've just called `gallery_mc`) with the `loadMovie` command. Select the keyframe in the `scripts` layer under the `gallery` label. Add a line of code above the `stop();` action already there:

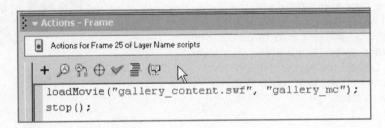

```
loadMovie("gallery_content.swf", "gallery_mc");
stop();
```

3. Save your movie and test it. Your movie should now look like the one shown here, with the gallery loaded into the middle strip, but with the buttons along the top working. You'll be able to see the pictures on either side of your main Flash stage –

don't worry; you won't be able to see that
in your final Flash presentation.

4. Now that we've done this once, and you've
   seen how easy it is, we need to do it for our
   about page. Select the keyframe under the
   about label in the about layer, and drag an
   instance of our placeholder movie clip into
   it. Give it an instance name of about_mc,
   and position it at (0, 131).

5. Select the keyframe in the script layer
   underneath the about label, and bring up
   the Actions panel. We're going to use the
   exact same way of loading in about_con-
   tent.swf, so enter the following:

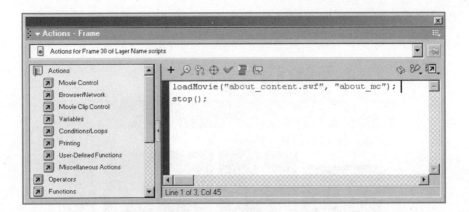

6. Save your movie and test it. You should be used to this method by now, so select the keyframe under the `contact` label in the `contact` layer, and drag an instance of our placeholder movie clip into it. Give it an instance name of `contact_mc`, and position it at (0,131). Now select the keyframe in the `script` layer underneath the `contact` label, and add the following line:

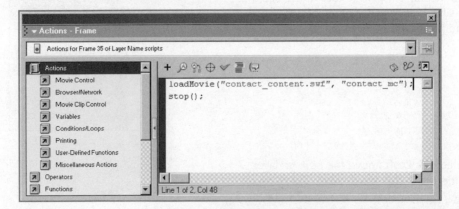

7. Save the movie and test. Your timeline should look like this.

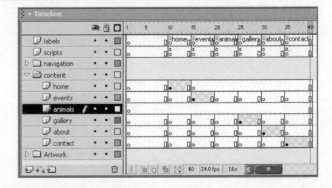

The "animal details" SWF

You might be thinking that all this loading in is unnecessarily complex, but it makes sure that the content is only loaded in when the user wants it, ensuring that there are no unnecessary downloads. We've left the biggest SWF – the animal details – to last, as it's a little more complex.

Remember the movie that we set up to display random animal pictures and linked to it at the start of the session? Those links have got to go to work at any time, so we've got to make sure our animal details SWF is loaded in ready for whenever anyone clicks on one of those buttons for more information.

1. We'll set up the movie clip to provide the random images first. Select the frame underneath the `home` label in the `home` layer, and drag an instance of our trusty placeholder movie clip onto the stage. Give it an instance name of `random_mc`, and position it at (375, 140) so that our random animal picture will show to the right of the welcome text.

2. Select the frame underneath the `home` label in the `animal` layer, and drag another instance of the placeholder movie clip into it. Give it the instance name `animal_mc` and position it at (900, 900). We don't want to see the movie clip – we just want to load it up so that we can ask for content from it – so we position it somewhere that the viewer can't see.

3. Still on the `animals` layer, select Insert > Clear Keyframe to remove the keyframe from frame 15 (underneath the `events` label). In frame 20, underneath the `animals` label, add another instance of our placeholder movie clip at (0,131), and give it the instance name `animal_mc`.

4. In the `scripts` layer, select the keyframe underneath the `home` label. We want to load our random images SWF (`smalls.swf`), and our animal content SWF (`animal_content.swf`). Enter these two lines above the `stop();` action:

5. When we get to `animal_content` SWF, we need to know whether the user got there by asking for more information on one of the random pictures, or if they just pressed the `animals` button. We need to know this because if they got there by the first method, we need to take them immediately to the right frame label to show them the animal they clicked on, but if they got there the second way, we can just play the movie clip as normal. We've just set `animalTarget` to remember if someone asked for more details on one of the random pictures, so our first step will be to ask `animalTarget` if this happened. Select the frame under the `animals` label on the scripts layer, and enter:

```
if(animalTarget != "none") {
```

> `!=` *is another way of saying "is not equal to" in ActionScript, so here we're saying if* `animalTarget` *isn't* none, *then do this...*

6. In the last session, we set `animalText` to the name of the animal when the person pressed the button, so we can simply tell `animal_mc` to and go to the frame with that label name. Say someone asked for more information on the tiger, then `animalTarget` would remember this, and we can tell `animal_content` to go to the `tiger` label, which contains our tiger information. To tell the `animal_content` SWF to go to the animal name stored in `animalTarget`, enter this line:

```
animal_mc.gotoAndStop(animalTarget);
```

7. Once we've seen the animal's details, we can reset `animalTarget` to none, so that when our visitor comes back to the animals gallery, they won't see the same animal again. Enter this:

```
animalTarget = "none";
```

8. We've told the Flash player what to do if someone had got there by clicking on one of our random animal pictures. If they just got there by clicking the animals button on the navigation (in which case `animalTarget` will be set to none), then we want the movie clip to play as normal. Enter the following:

```
} else {
    animal_mc.gotoAndPlay(1);
}
```

9. Check that your full script looks like this, and save the file – we'll test it in a moment, after we've added the audio.

Actions - Frame

Actions for Frame 20 of Layer Name scripts

```
if(animalTarget != "none") {
    animal_mc.gotoAndStop(animalTarget);
    animalTarget = "none";
} else {
    animal_mc.gotoAndPlay(1);
}
stop();
```

Loading the audio

There is one other thing to load in: our audio track. When loading SWFs into another SWF, we have two options. We can load them into a target movie clip, which is what we've just done, or we can load them into a **level**.

In Flash, you can load things in on levels, and these will appear over each other, just like putting transparencies on a projector. The main timeline of your movie will be loaded in by Flash at level 0, and anything else you load in goes above that. We are going to bring our audio into level 100, so it's well away from anything else. You don't need to have the intermediate levels (1-99) filled in. By choosing such a high number you don't have to worry about how many levels you've already used loading in various movies. You can pretty much assume level 100 won't be taken.

1. Open up the PAWS file again. Select the home layer's frame under the home label. This is where we loaded `smalls.swf` and `animal_content.swf`, and it's where we will load our audio track. Add the following line of code just before the `stop();` command:

```
loadMovie("audio.swf", 100);
```

Actions - Frame

Actions for Frame 10 of Layer Name scripts

```
1  loadMovie("smalls.swf", "random_mc");
2  loadMovie("animal_content.swf", "animal_mc");
3  loadMovie("audio.swf", 100);
4  stop();
5
```

2. Save the file. Make sure that the audio file
    you created in Session 6 – `audio.swf` – is
    in the same place as your PAWS file, and
    test it. The audio should play, and you
    should be able to switch it on and off with
    the button in the bottom right-hand corner
    of your main screen.

Testing, testing

Lets give our Flash movie a solid test.

1. Close Flash, and find the SWF for the latest
    version of the PAWS file you've been work-
    ing on. Double-click on it to launch it in the
    Flash Player. When it starts up, you should
    get a random animal on the front page.
    Check that the link for more information
    works here – if you get one of the animals
    without a link for information, just close the
    Flash Player and double-click your SWF
    again.

2. Go to the `animals` page if you didn't get the tiger on the front page, and check that the video works.

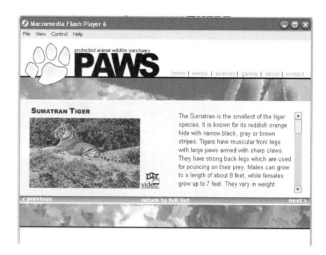

3. Check the `events` page: this section of the site contains text loaded in from an external text file. This means the client can change the text without having to do anything with Flash. We can check just how dynamic this is. Leave your SWF running in the Flash Player, and open up `text.txt` in Notepad or SimpleText. Alter the text to a new event, but make sure you haven't changed the `&eventText=` and the `&` at the end. Save your file, go to another section (watch your car drive down the street on the `contact` page, for example), and come back. Hey presto! Your new information is there.

Further steps

Congratulations: our PAWS site is now up and running. In the next few sessions, we'll be polishing our site, adding some random effects and transitions before taking a look at optimizing everything so that it's as perfect as it can be for the web.

The potential for using what you've learned in this chapter elsewhere is huge. You've seen how easy it is to load content into a Flash movie from other places, now think how easy this makes changing or updating content, or how easy it is to manage Flash sites with a lot of information or large files when you can simply load in a SWF for each different subject. Try taking the random pictures script and creating your own random home page.

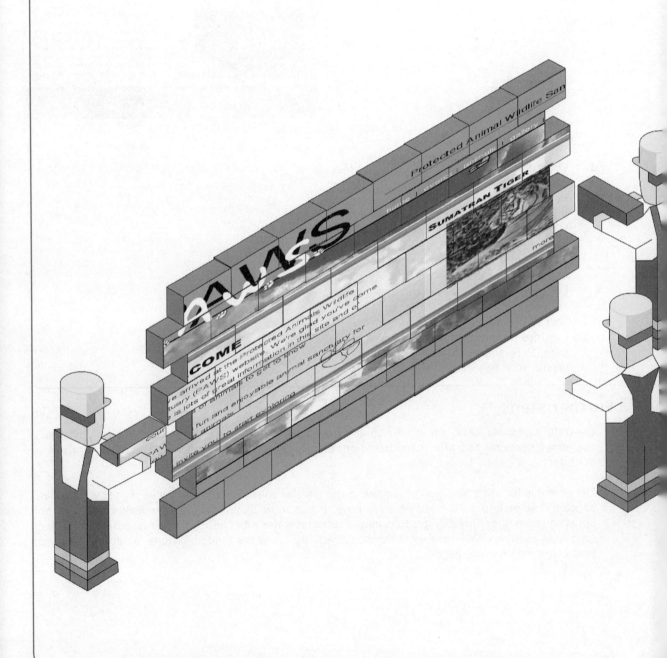

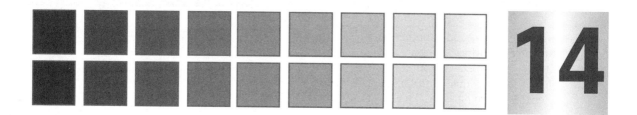

Transitions and Random Effects

We've done all the hard work. The site is pretty much up and running, so now's the time to add a few extra touches before we do our final loading assembly of the site in the next session. We're going to:

- Add an animation (or **transition**) to load our main background image in smoothly
- Create some ActionScript to run our random effects

1. We're going to create a preloader in the next session, and we'll use a transition to move from the preloader to the home page. Open the PAWS movie, `paws_006.fla`, and close all the layer folders, then open the `artwork` folder. In the `lines` layer, add a keyframe to the second frame, draw a line, and position it near the center of the stage.

2. Insert a keyframe in frame 3 and, using the Free Transform tool, extend the line so it reaches across the stage. Next modify the line with the Arrow tool so that it bends upwards.

3. Create a blank keyframe in frame 4. Copy the curve from the previous frame and paste it in place. Use the Transform panel to rotate it 180 degrees so that it curves the other way.

4. In the next frame, add another blank keyframe, and drag an instance of `black_line_size_3` from the Library and align it to the center of the stage so it forms a lens like opening.

5. Add a blank keyframe to frame 7. In frame 7, drag two instances of `black_line_size_3` from the Library and position them at (-8, 160), and (-8, 320).

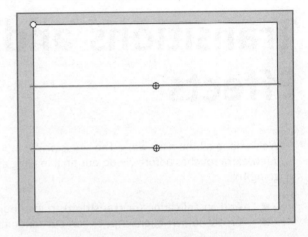

6. In frame 9, add a keyframe, and adjust the positions of the two lines to (-8, 100) and (-8, 380). Test your movie. We've a line arriving, bending and splitting to reveal content beneath.

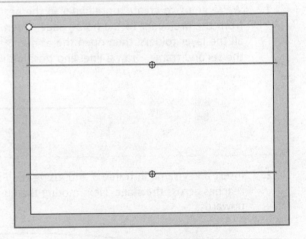

7. We've set up the transition, but we need to set how we're going to reveal the content. We'll do this with a **mask**. Add a new layer, call it `Mask`, and drag it above `red_02`, the layer with our main background image. We'll use this as a mask layer, so right-click on the layer name, and select `mask`.

8. Creating the mask layer should automatically change `red_02` to a **masked** layer (the layer will be indented and the layer symbol will have changed). If it hasn't changed automatically, you can manually make the layer masked by right-clicking on the layer name, and then selecting `Masked` from the dialog box that appears when you choose the `Properties` option.

9. In the `red_02` layer, drag the keyframe from frame 10 to frame 7. In the `Mask` layer, create a keyframe in frame 7, and draw a rectangle that fits between the two black lines we animated earlier. My rectangle is pink: it doesn't matter what color a mask is, as it's never seen: the rectangle defines the area that is seen by the user. Imagine cutting a rectangle out of a sheet of paper; this is a mask. You only see what's visible through the hole in the paper.

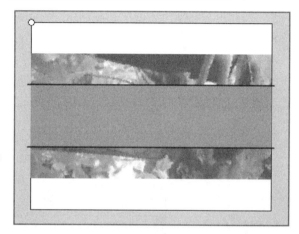

10. Add a keyframe to frame 9 of the `Mask` layer, and scale the rectangle shape to fit between the lines. Finish off by adding a blank keyframe at frame 10 of the `Mask` layer. Lock both the mask and masked layers.

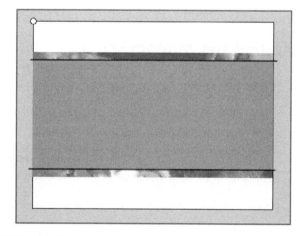

11. Save your movie and test it. You should see your lines part to reveal the background image, although this will happen a little more quickly when you test it locally than on a server. It's essential that the two layers are both locked or the mask won't work.

Adding our random effects into the PAWS site

1. If you can remember the early sessions, we have some animations that we want to randomly appear on stage. We saved them in `random_effects.fla`. Create a new layer in the PAWS movie, call it `effects`, and drag it so that it's above the other layers. Drag an instance of `place-holder` onto the stage, give it an instance name of `random_mc`, and place it at (0,0).

2. As you may or may not have discovered, there's one snag with the `audio.swf` we loaded into our site in the last session: if you turn the audio off, and return to the home page, it starts again. This could be really irritating, so add a keyframe in frame 5 of the scripts layer. Select frame 1 of the `scripts` layer, and cut:

    ```
    loadMovie("audio.swf", 100);
    ```

3. Paste this into the keyframe you've just added on frame 5, and add the following line to load in our random effects:

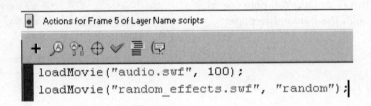

Adding the random scripts

We've loaded the content; now we need a script to run the effects. We've already made sure that our bird calls play randomly, and now we'll make our animations play randomly, but not too often. Our animations take roughly three seconds to play, and we certainly don't want more than one to play at a time. We only need four lines of code to make this random animation effect very pleasing, with a different animation playing intermittently and not too often. Used sparingly, this is a very nice effect. We will use an **array** to achieve this random effect. An array is a container for storing information. For example, in an array called `lunchBox` we'll store our lunch:

```
lunchBox = ["sandwich","chips","lemonade"]
```

The quotes are only necessary with certain types of values. Arrays are automatically numbered, starting with 0, so in the `lunchBox` array, `lunchBox[0]` is "sandwich", `lunchBox[1]` is "chips" and `lunchBox[2]` is "lemonade".

Random numbers work particularly well with arrays, because you can come up with a random number that will then match something in your array, leading to random images, random quotes, that sort of thing. Arrays are a very powerful part of ActionScript, and pretty easy to work with.

Open up `random_effects.fla` – either use the version from the CD, or make sure that your version has the following:

- Two instances of the leaf and butterfly animations, each on separate layers on the main timeline with the instance names `butterfly_01`, `butterfly_02`, `leaf_01`, and `leaf_02`.
- All four layers containing these animations extended to last 160 frames.
- `Stop();` actions added to the first frame of each animation. In the case of the `leaf_collection` animation, you'll need to move all the other content to frame 2 in order to prevent the leaf making an unwelcome appearance on the edge of the stage.

---

1. We'll make an array of our animation movie clips. Add a layer called `scripts`, select the first frame, and add this script:

```
choices=[leaf_01,leaf_02,butterfly_01,butterfly_02]
```

Note there are no quotes around the movie clip instance names here. `choices` is the name of the array, and we've got the instance names of the clips as the content. Make sure you've named your movie clips with these names, or it won't work.

---

2. We don't want our animations to constantly play, because it would be too hectic, and the viewer would pick up on the rhythm of the repetition. But if we get a random number that's bigger than the number of choices we have in our array, Flash will be asked to play a movie clip that doesn't exist, and we'll be able to space out our animations. We'll assign that random number to a variable, `myrando`, which you can change as you wish. Add to your code:

```
myrando=8;
```

---

3. This isn't a random number yet, just a value to work with. Next we'll type:

```
playit = Math.ceil(Math.random()*myrando)-1;
```

This chooses a random number between 0 and 7 and stores it as the variable `playit`. Let's quickly look at what's happening here. `Math.random()` produces a value between 0 and 1. We multiply it by `myrando` to get a value between 0 and 8. This random value could be a decimal, and we want an integer, so we use the `Math.ceil` method, which rounds the value *up* to the nearest integer. This gives a value between 1 and 8. We finally subtract 1 from this value to give us a random number between 0 and 7 – remember, arrays start at 0 rather than 1.

---

4. Now add:

```
choices[playit].play();
```

This commands Flash to play the array item (a movie clip in our case) located at position `playit` to play. So if your random number was 3, the movie clip `butterfly_02` would play as it is number 3 in the array.

The way we get our intermittent playing is by making that `rando` number bigger than the number of items in the array, so sometimes the Flash player is asked to play an array item that doesn't exist. Thus we get empty time on the screen. This means we don't have an annoying constantly repeating series of animations.

That's it. That's all the code you need!

5. Here's the code for frame 1 in full:

```
choices = [leaf_01, leaf_02,
butterfly_01, butterfly_02];
myrando = 8;
playit =
Math.ceil(Math.random()*myrando)-
1;
choices[playit].play();
```

6. Okay, publish the random effects movie now, and then close it – we've now got the SWF that will load into the PAWS movie. Go back to the main PAWS movie and test that now. You should see your animation floating above the site seemingly at random. If you want to see the animation more frequently, make `myrando` a number between 3 and 8, but remember, people come to your site for information, and may find too much top-level animation just gets in the way. If you want to see the animation less often, make `myrando` greater than 8. Experiment.

Adding our random audio

Back in session 6, you'll remember that we set up `birdCalls_random.fla` ready to play our random sounds. We've now got to add a few labels to that file, and a bit of script to the `audio.fla` file to make this happen.

1. Open up `birdCalls_random.fla`. Your timeline should look like the one shown – one layer, with a blank keyframe in the first frame, and your `birdcall_01 – 04` movie clips on the next four frames. Add a `stop();` action to the blank keyframe in frame 1.

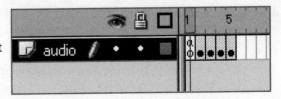

2. Open `audio.fla`, and add a new layer called `random`. Add blank keyframes to the first two frames.

3. Create a new movie clip, and call it `random`. Don't add anything to it – we'll use this as a placeholder to load `birdcalls_random.swf` into. Drag the empty movie clip into the first frame of the `random` layer, and position it in the top left-hand corner. Give it the instance name of `random` in the Property inspector.

4. To load `birdCalls_random` into this placeholder, select the first frame of the scripts layer, and add the line `loadMovie("birdCalls_random.swf", "random");` before the `stop();` action already there.

```
loadMovie("birdCalls_random.swf", "random");
stop();
```

5. Now select the instance of `random` on the stage, and bring up the Actions window. Add:

```
onClipEvent(load){
freq = 900;
}

onClipEvent(enterFrame){
frameNum = Math.round(random(freq));
if(frameNum <= 5){ gotoAndStop(frameNum);
    }
}
```

What's going on here? As soon as the movie loads, we set the frequency with which we want our random sounds to play. Every time Flash enters a frame (24 times a second), we get a random value from 900 with random(freq), and turn this into a whole number with `Math.round` (decimal frame numbers aren't going to help!). If it's equal to, or less than 5 (remember that our sounds are on frames 2 to 5), we tell Flash to play that frame in `birdCalls_random.fla`.

6. Close the Actions window, and save your file.

Further steps

We've created our site, added transitions, and some random effects. All we've left to do is learn about optimizing the file and getting it ready to upload onto the web, and we're there.

Meanwhile, there are plenty of ways you can customize what we've done here. Want to change the animations, or add some more now that you can see them play as part of the main site? You can use our array method and add as many animations as you want without it feeling too crowded, as long as you always make the `myrando` number larger than the number of items in your array.

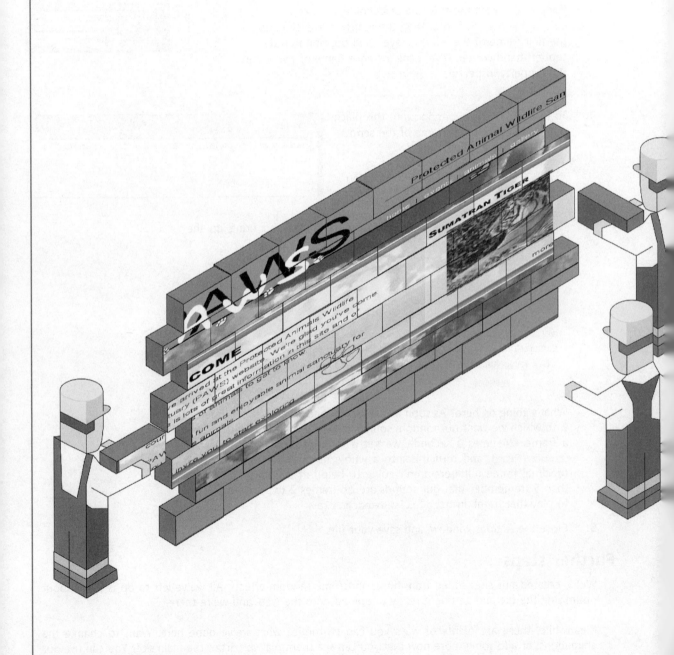

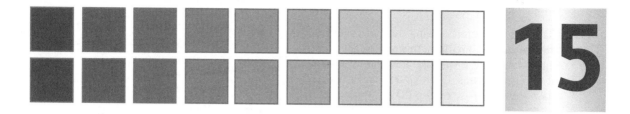

Optimization and Preloaders

We've built our site, and it's functioning as it should. Now we need to make sure that our site is easy to access, and the number one problem with accessing content on the web is download times. At the moment, everything runs fine, and everything happens instantaneously; but the moment we upload anything to the server, the length of time taken to download our site will depend on the size of the file, the speed of the server, and the speed of the connection: plenty to go wrong.

We're going to address this issue by creating a preloader to add to any of our files that exceed 20KB. What is a preloader? It serves two purposes. Firstly, when a user selects something that takes time to load, it tells them what's going on. Just give the user a blank screen, and they're not going to think something's loading, they're going to think something's gone wrong.

Secondly, a preloader makes sure that the movie doesn't start playing until it's fully loaded, making sure that the movie doesn't stop, start, stop, start again, and so on. Because you can't tell how long they're going to have to play, preloaders are usually a loop that keeps on looping until the site loads.

Before we add our preloader, let's get an accurate picture of how long our site is going to take to load.

1. Flash has a tool for working this out called the **Bandwidth Profiler**. This graphically shows how long it will take for a file to load at different speeds. Open your main PAWS Flash movie, (saved on the CD as `PAWS_007.fla`) and test it. While it's testing, select View > Bandwidth Profiler. Bring up the View menu again, and select Streaming Graph. On the left of this, you can immediately see details like the movie's size, frame rate, duration, and more.

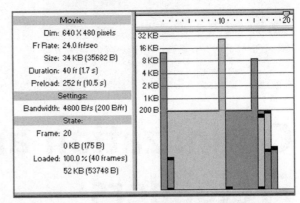

2. By default, Flash shows you loading speeds for the 56k modem that we said at the beginning of our book would be used by our typical visitor. Try going to the Debug menu, selecting a different speed, and selecting Control > Play to load the movie again.

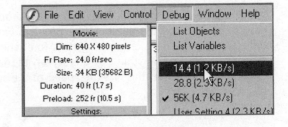

3. Across the top of the Bandwidth Profiler, you can see the frame numbers on the Flash timeline. The bar graph effect underneath shows us how much we need to load in for each frame, and the red line shows us how much we can load in. If we go above the red line, we're in trouble... oops. Time to build a preloader.

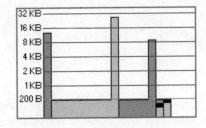

> The Bandwidth Profiler is only a simulation, and is not as accurate as testing in real world situations.

4. In the main PAWS file, add a new layer below the `scripts` layer, and call it `preloader`. Drag an instance of `logo_outline` onto the stage, scale it to 50% with the Transform panel, break it apart (Modify > Break Apart), select it, and convert it to a movie clip called `logo_pre-loader`.

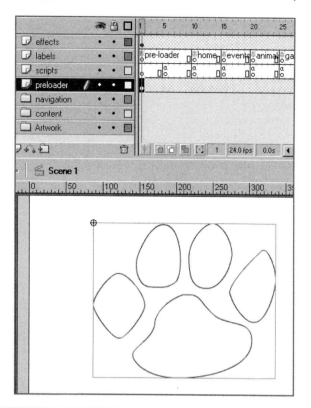

5. Double-click on your new movie clip to edit it in place. Rename the default layer out-line, and add a new layer called text.

6. Select the Text tool. In the Property inspector select font size 40, Arial Black, and set it to Dynamic Text. In the first frame of the text layer, add 00 to the middle of the paw print. Give the text field the instance name percentLoadText.

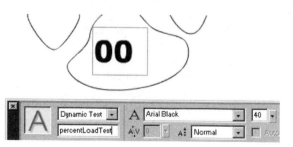

7. In the same frame, de-select the text field you've just created. Set the font size in the Property inspector back to 30, and choose `Static Text`. Create a new text field, and type in a percentage symbol. Place this next to the other text field.

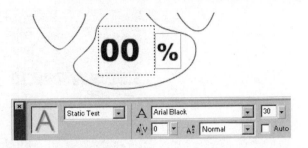

8. Return to the main timeline, and give your movie clip an instance name of `preLoader`. Center it to the stage horizontally and vertically using the Align panel.

9. Add a blank keyframe to the second frame in this layer, so that the preloader only exists in the first frame.

10. Now comes the tricky part – writing the script to do the preloading. Select the first frame on the `scripts` layer, and open the Actions panel. We want something to happen when Flash enters the frame with our movie clip (instance name `preLoader`, remember) on it, so enter:

```
preLoader.onEnterFrame = function
() {
```

11. Next, we want to store some information for us to work out our percentages from. To do this we need to know the amount of the movie that has loaded and the total size of the movie. We can use `getBytesLoaded`, and `getBytesTotal` to do this in Flash, so we'll store these values in `bytesLoaded` and `bytesTotal`. Add these next two lines:

```
bytesLoaded = getBytesLoaded();
bytesTotal = getBytesTotal();
```

12. Now that we've got the size of our movie stored in `bytesTotal`, we can check to see if there is anything in our movie to load or not. If there is, then `bytesTotal`'s value will be greater than –1, so add:

```
if (bytesTotal > -1) {
```

13. Now comes the math. We've got our values already, so I'm sure that you won't be surprised to learn that we're going to work out the percent loaded by dividing `bytesLoaded` by `bytesTotal`. Add:

```
percent = bytesLoaded/bytesTotal;
```

14. The results from this are going to be a little bit messy, so we need to do two things. We need to convert the result from a decimal to a number between 1 and 100, and we need to round the result off so that we get a two-digit figure to fit in our paw print. We can use `Math.round` to round our figure off, before multiplying by 100 to convert from a decimal to a number between 1 and 100. Enter:

```
percentage = Math.round(percent*100);
```

15. We've got our percentage value sorted, so we can send it to the text field that we created earlier to be displayed to the user. We need tell Flash to look for our percent load text in the preloader movie clip instance we specified at the beginning of the script. We can use the `this` command to refer to the same preloader movie clip, so add:

```
this.percentLoadText.text = percentage;
```

16. That's almost it, but we need to somehow stop when we reach 100%. If the percentage is greater than 99, we need to stop things. We're going to do this by hiding the movie clip – just as we set x and y positions for movie clips earlier, we can also set their visibility to `true` or `false`. Enter:

```
if (percentage >= 99) {
this._visible = false;
```

17. We've now hidden the preloader, so we need to play the main content. This will be on the root timeline, so add:

```
_root.gotoAndPlay(2);
```

18. Add three `}`'s to close everything off, with a carriage return after each. Add a `stop();` at the bottom to prevent Flash moving off this frame until we've told it to (when percentage equals more than 99). Check your code against the screenshot.

```
preLoader.onEnterFrame = function () {
    bytesLoaded = getBytesLoaded();
    bytesTotal = getBytesTotal();
    if (bytesTotal > -1) {
        percent = bytesLoaded/bytesTotal;
        percentage = Math.round(percent*100);
        this.percentLoadText.text = percentage;
        if (percentage >= 99) {
            this._visible = false;
            _root.gotoAndPlay(2);
        }
    }
}
stop();
```

Line 14 of 16, Col 8

19. Save your movie and test it. Once the movie is playing, go to the View menu and select Show Streaming – this allows Flash to simulate the streaming environment. You should be rewarded with your paw counting up the percentage values. Don't worry if this has all left you a bit confused: what's good is that you can now use this preloader anytime you need a preloader in Flash. (If you try to test in a browser or without showing streaming, you won't see anything. This is because the files load incredibly quickly off the hard drive.)

20. If you remember looking at the Bandwidth Profiler earlier, there was nothing indicated after frame 20 because all the other content was being loaded in from other SWFs. We need to add preloaders to these, as they actually contain more content than the main Flash movie. Select the first frame of the `preloader` layer, which contains our movie clip, and copy it.

21. Open `about_content.fla`. Create blank keyframes in frame 5 of all four layers, and move the content on frame 1 of each layer to the new keyframes. Create a new layer called `preloader`, add a blank keyframe to the second frame. Paste in the movie clip that we've just copied at frame 1.

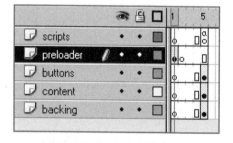

22. Back in the main PAWS file, select the first frame, open the Actions panel and select the preloader code we added earlier. Copy this, and swap back to `about_content.fla`. Create a blank key frame in the first frame of the `scripts` layer, and paste the code into the first frame.

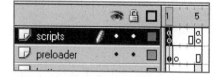

23. There is something we need to alter. If we were to load our preloader when the user asks for `about_content`, then the script will run `_root.gotoAndPlay(2);`. We don't want the main PAWS movie to go to frame 2, we want our `about_content` movie clip to go to frame 2. In the pre-loader script for `about_content`, change `_root.gotoAndPlay(2);` to:

```
_level0.about_mc.gotoAndPlay(2);
```

```
if (percentage >= 99) {
        this._visible = false;
        _level0.about_mc.gotoAndPlay(2);
    }
  }
}
stop();
```

> `_level0` and `_root` *are the same thing within an individual movie; they are the master level at the top of the movie's structure.*

24. Flash will just loop through the timeline if we don't tell it otherwise, and the last thing we want is to play our preloader over and over again. Add a `stop();` action to the end of the script on frame 5 of the `scripts` layer

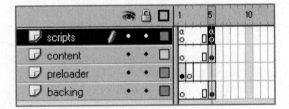

25. Save your movie. If you test it, it won't work anymore, but that's what we want. Swap back to the main PAWS movie and test that. If you go to the `about` section, you should see your preloader in action – note it will probably only flash very quickly before your eyes, as the file is loaded from the hard drive in an instant.

26. Now copy the preloader frame and script into the files listed below, changing the script as we have just done, with the relevant movie clip instance name. You don't need to preload the audio because:

- The audio is going to load in when it can – it's not crucial to the content.
- The audio being set to stream will play as it arrives.

File Name to add preloader to
```
About_content.fla
Animal_content.fla
Contact_content.fla
Gallery_content.fla
```

Code Change to preloader script in frame 1
```
_level0.about_mc.gotoAndPlay(2);
_level0.animal_mc.gotoAndPlay(2);
_level0.contact_mc.gotoAndPlay(2);
_level0.gallery_mc.gotoAndPlay(2);
```

27. Before we finish, one last step to help our movie load in even easier. Components like the scrollbar we've used can be a great help, but they're set up to export from the Library in the first frame, adding extra download time just when we want everything cleared out of the way so that our preloader can work. Our scrollbar, for example, is 16KB and will load in before the rest of the file unless we turn it off. To do this, open up your Library, and find the Flash UI Component folder.

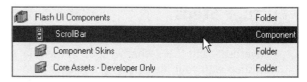

28. Right-click on the Scrollbar component, and select Properties. Click on the Advanced button (to the left of the Help button). Uncheck the Export in first frame button, and hit OK.

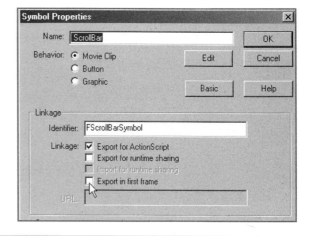

29. Still in the Library, inside the Core Assets folder, open the FUIComponent Class Tree folder. Select the FUIComponent, and right-click on it. Select Properties again, and uncheck the Export in first frame option. Be careful not to change anything else, or you scrollbar might mysteriously stop working.

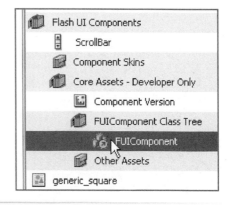

30. Save the file and test it – if you run the Bandwidth Profiler, you will see that the first frame is now sitting around the 8kb mark, which is much better.

Further Steps

Congratulations! That's our PAWS site finished. It only remains for us to publish, upload to the web, and advertise – and that's what we'll do in the final session. It's a good idea to recognize the fact that you've finished with your file by saving a final version – we've called ours `PAWS_master.fla`.

This session hasn't only shown you how to add a preloader to the PAWS site, it's shown you how to create a preloader that you could use anywhere. If you've got any big Flash movies – particularly those with a lot of imported artwork or video in them – try going and adding a preloader to them now. You'll probably want to change the paw print for a slightly more suitable graphic - make sure that the graphic you use instead is small enough for the preloader to load in instantly, otherwise you'll end up creating a preloader for the preloader, and that's not good...

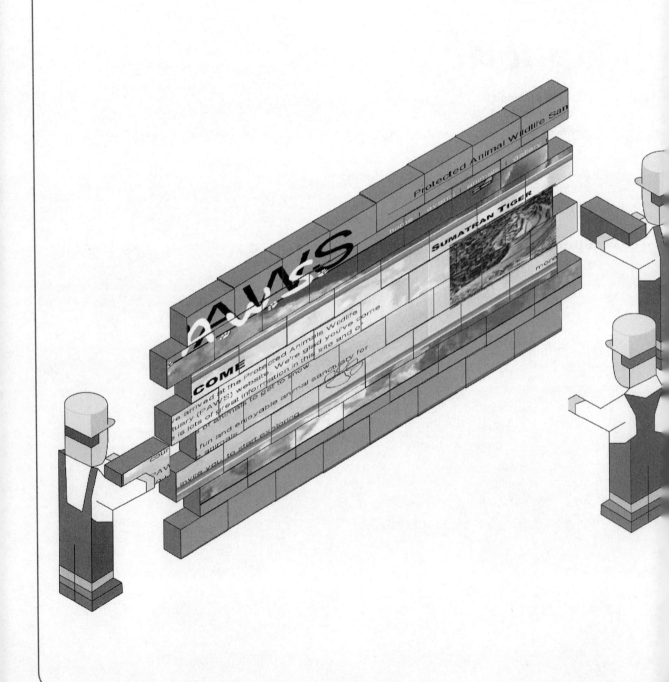

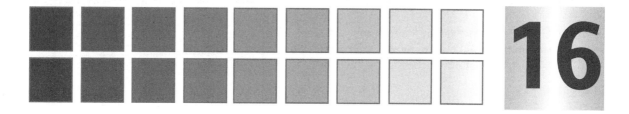

From Hard Disk to Web

Your site is completed, and you've gained mastery over Flash. Most books would leave you right here, but we don't think that's really fair. At the moment, your site is completed, but it's still sitting on your local drive. You need to get it on the web, and you need to let people know about it. That's what this session is all about.

We're also going to take a look at working out who's visiting your site, so that you can see whether the assumptions about our users that we set out at the beginning of the book are correct, and modify your site/promotion strategies accordingly.

Preparing our files for the web

1. First, we need to **publish** our Flash Movie. Open PAWS_master.fla (or your version of the final PAWS file), and go to File > Publish Settings. We want to export a .SWF file, but we also want to export an .HTML file for the SWF to sit inside in a browser, so check these two.

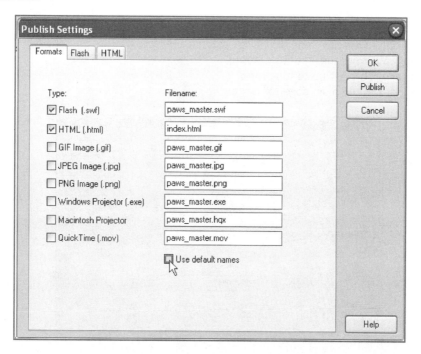

2.   Click on the HTML tab at the top, and choose the Flash with Named Anchors template so that our anchors work.

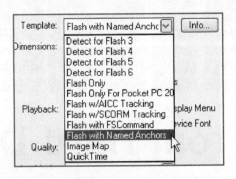

3.   Leave the Dimensions setting as Match Movie: we have some bitmap content, so allowing the movie to be scaled would mean a user could distort the images by scaling it to a different size. Under playback, uncheck the display menu option. Usually, if you right-click on a Flash movie whilst it's running, you'll get a menu offering you the chance to go forward or backwards, and zoom in. This makes sure our users don't get to see this menu.

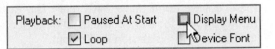

4.   The rest of the default settings are fine, so move onto the formats tab. Uncheck the Use default names option at the bottom, and change the HTML file name to index.html. We're changing this because most web servers are set up to look for a file called index as the main page for a site.

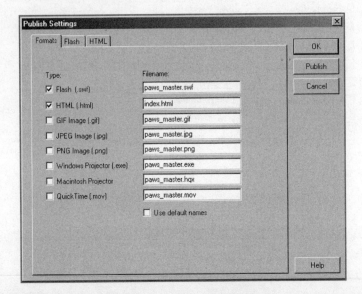

5. Hit `Publish`, save the movie, and exit Flash. Create a folder called `upload_to_web`, and copy all your SWFs into it, along with `index.html`.

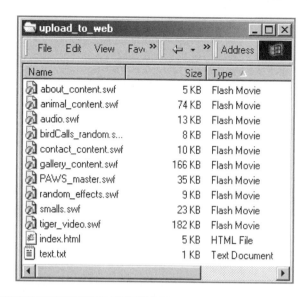

6. Double-click `index.html` to open it in your browser and your Flash movie should play. Try all the buttons and make sure they work. Windows users with Internet Explorer 6 (Help > About Internet Explorer will tell you which version you have if you're not sure) can try using their back button to see if our named anchors work as well.

7. We also want to create a CD version of the PAWS site to send to local schools and other interested parties. To play a Flash file without using a browser with a Flash plug-in do this, we need to create a **Projector** file. Start by creating a new folder on your machine, and calling it `publish_cd`. Copy all the files apart from `index.html` from your `upload_to_web` folder and into this one.

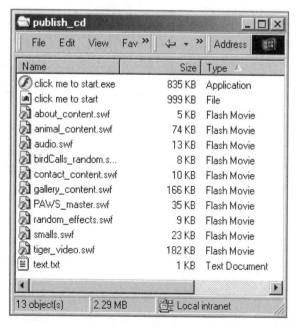

209

8. Back in the PAWS file, go to File > Publish
Settings again, and uncheck the SWF and
HTML options we checked earlier. You want
to check the option for the platform you're
using here – Mac or PC. A PC should recognize any file with an .exe extension, but
Macs are a little different. To make them
recognize that our Projector file is a Flash
Projector document, we have to create a
HQX file here, that a Mac can uncompress
and label as a Flash Projector document
when it does that. If you want to burn a CD
that works on both platforms, you'll need to
use a Mac anyway, so unpack the HQX file
on the Mac before burning it to the CD.

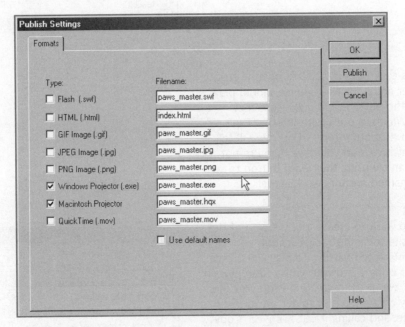

9. Hit Publish to generate the files, and move
these to your publish_cd folder. Double-
click on whichever file is relevant to your
platform, and you'll see your site come up
not in your web browser, but in the Flash
Player.

> *WARNING! When we were testing this, we found that creating the Mac Projector on our PCs frequently caused Flash to crash – the* Publishing *dialog window would come up, and stop a few bars short of complete. This seems to be mainly an issue on machines that are a bit short on RAM, but don't worry: even if Flash does crash, the files will be created and will work fine. Just make sure you save before you create your Projector files...*

10. You could now burn this folder to CD. Before you do this, you need to give the user some way of easily working out how to run the PAWS site. There are a number of ways to do this: you could set the CD to autorun when you burn it, you could add a readme.txt file with instructions, or you could make a label for the front of the CD box reading Double-click on PAWS to run. The simplest and best method is probably to uncheck the Use Default Names option in the Publish settings box, and rename the EXE and HQX files Click Me to Start.

| ☑ Windows Projector (.exe) | click me to start.exe |
| ☑ Macintosh Projector | click me to start.hqx |

Moving our files onto the web

To put our files up on the web, we need some server space. Many of you probably have a small amount of web space provided with your internet connection, which is ideal for our purposes. Otherwise, go to google.com, and do a search for free hosting – places like brinkster.com, geocities.com, and freeservers.com are among the free hosts out there.

As your site becomes more complex, and your visitor numbers increase, you will want to start to look at professional, paid hosts like duramedia.net, burlee.com, web-side.com, and mediatemple.net. You probably don't want to do this yet, and - as with everything else in life - prices and services will vary. Features to look out for are:

- the amount of storage offered
- the amount of data transfer per month
- ftp access
- support services (usually email or phone)

A professional paid service will also allow you to buy a custom domain name (a few free services allow you to direct a domain name to them, but not many). Registering a domain name is likely to cost around US$10 or equivalent these days. There are lots of places where you can buy a domain (www.registerfly.com, and www.dotster.com, for example), and more and more hosting companies are offering domain registration as part of their hosting packages.

The key here is to find a memorable domain name that people will remember. www.paws.com is great, www.protectedanimalwildlifesanctuary.com is too long - imagine trying to email dave@protectedanimalwildlifesanctuary.com without making a mistake.

With two of the free hosts named above, you'll be able to upload your files by using the online uploading facilities that you can access once you've got your username and password confirmed (you can see the geocitites menu above, and the brinkster one below).

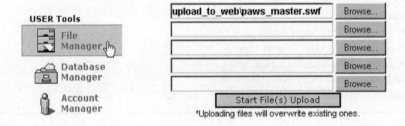

If you're not given the option of uploading files straight into your web space like this, then you need to use a FTP program to move the files from your local drive to your web space. With commercial hosts, or the space free you get with your ISP, you'll also need to use an FTP program.

Fortunately, these are quite easy to use, and we've included trial versions of Cute (for PC) and Fetch (for Mac) on the CD with this book. Once you've installed these in the usual way, start your FTP program up. Both Fetch and Cute will ask you for host, ID and password at the start, and you'll need to use ftp.yourhost.com, and the username and password you registered with there. Cute

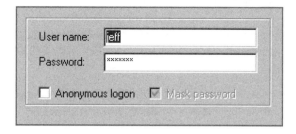

Once you've entered these details and the FTP program has connected, create a new folder called `paws`, and move the files from the `upload_to_web` directory into it. Open up the URL for your account, add `/paws` to the end of it, and your `index.html` file should load up. You've made it - you've got a fully functioning professional Flash site up and running and on the web. It's difficult to underline how much you've learned and covered by this stage, but it's a real achievement: well done.

It's difficult to give any more specific instructions without knowing what FTP software or host you're using. If you do hit problems, check out the Help sections at fetchsoftworks.com *or* www.cuteftp.com. *If you're still not getting anywhere, come and post in the forum, and there should be someone else there using the same host/ftp combination who can offer some advice.*

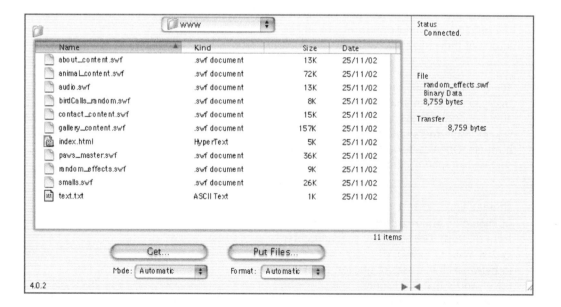

Adding your site to a search engine

Your site is up and running, but this isn't much good if no one can see the results of your hard work. The best way to get your site visited is to tell people it's there - print the URL on any correspondence, put it in your email, and share links with others. Approach like-minded sites and see if they would be interested in a link swap.

We're going to look at two other ways to raise the profile of your site: making sure that search engines know that you're there, and including Flash advertising in email.

1.   We're going to start with looking at search engines, so head over to google.com/about.html and select the `sub-mitting your site` option under the `For Site Owners` section heading.

For Site Owners

Advertise with Us
Premium Sponsorships, AdWc

Search Solutions
Google Search Appliance, Wel

Webmaster Info
Dos & don'ts, Ranking questioi

Submitting yourSite
How Google adds URLs...

2.   On this page, you will find a small form that allows you to submit your web address to be "crawled" by the Google software robots and then added to Google's database. Add the URL, and a short description (Google's is the simplest of submission forms, others go into a lot more detail).

URL: http://www.paws.com

Comments: The offical site for PAWS - the protected anii

3.   Search engines sometimes use meta-data that you include in your HTML file to learn about it, and categorize it. This information is kept inside meta tags in the head of your html file. Open `index.html` in a text editor, such as Notepad or Simple Text.

4.   Find the line `<BODY bgcolor="#FFFFFF">` (it should be about a dozen lines down from the top). Create a new line, and enter `<meta name="keywords" content="">`. In between the last set of quotes, enter a list of words that hold some significance for the site, such as: `paws, tiger, lion, wildlife, protected, sanctuary`. Don't go overboard here: some search

engines will reject your site if it has over 50 words in.

```
index.html - Notepad                                    _□×
File  Edit  Format  Help
      function flashPutTitle(title) { document.title = title;
}
</script>
</HEAD>
<BODY bgcolor="#FFFFFF">
<meta name="keywords" content="paws, tiger, lion, wildlife,
protected, sanctuary">
<!-- URL's used in the movie-->
<!-- text used in the movie-->
<!--OO protected animal wildlife sanctuary□<P
```

Flash email signature

We've added our site to the search engines, so we're going to move on to create a Flash email banner. The key to these is to keep them small, and the Internet Advertising Bureau suggests a maximum size of 468x60 and 13kB as banner standards. Some forums don't allow them either, so be careful to check that they're OK before using them online.

1. Create a new Flash movie, give it a size of 468x60, and specify the usual 24 fps. Save this as `advert.fla`.

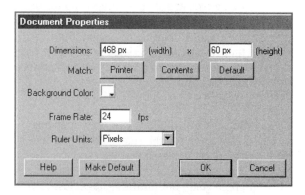

2. Rename the default layer `prints`, and open your PAWS movie as a library (File > Open as Library). Drag an instance of `logo_complete` onto the stage.

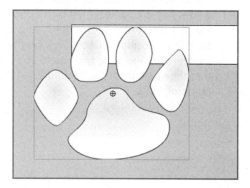

3. Use the Transform panel to scale this to `10%` and rotate it by 105 degrees. Place it at the top left of the stage.

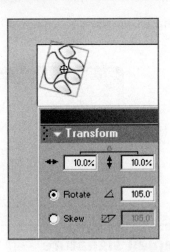

4. Select the print, and convert it to a movie clip called `walking`. Double-click to edit the movie clip in place. Add a keyframe at frame five, and drag another instance of `logo_complete` out of the library and onto the stage. Scale it to 10% again, but this time, rotate it by 75 degrees so that it faces inwards a little, to give the two footprints a natural look.

5. Select View > Rulers. Not only does this allow us to see the rulers along the sides of the stage, it means that we can click and hold over one of the rulers and drag a green guide out onto the stage. Just as with most Desktop Publishing software, these guides will not be included in the final Flash file that the viewer sees – they're just there to help us position things. Click on the horizontal ruler, and drag two rulers down so that they pass through the middle of the two footprints.

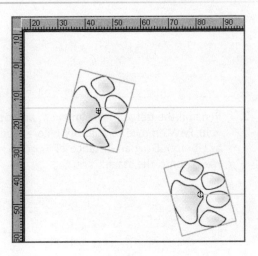

6. Add another keyframe five frames further on, drag another instance of `logo_complete` out of the library, scale and rotate it, and position it on the opposite side to the previous footprint. Do this until you reach frame 60, so that you have twelve footprints in all.

7. Your footprints will probably be placed slightly unevenly across the stage. This should give a natural feel, but if you feel that this doesn't work when you test your movie, use the Align panel to evenly space the footprints out on the last keyframe. Delete all the previous keyframes, add keyframes in again in the same places (this ensures all keyframes contain the updated location of the prints), and work back, deleting a footprint for each keyframe.

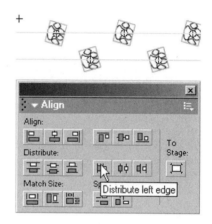

8. Add a new layer, call it scripts, and add a `stop();` action to the last frame.

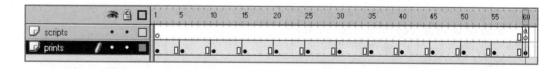

9. Return to the main timeline, and add keyframes to frames 50 and 60. Select the movie clip on the stage on frame 60, and choose `Tint` from the `Color:` drop-down in the Property inspector. Set this to 90%. Choose one of the frames between the keyframes on frames 50 and 60, and choose `Motion Tween` from the `Tween:` drop-down in the Property inspector. Test your

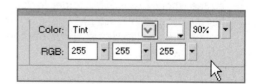

down in the Property inspector. Test your movie, and you should see your paw prints fading away as they reach the edge of the screen.

10. Add a new layer, and call it `text`. Add a keyframe to frame 50. Highlight this frame, and use the Text tool to enter `make tracks today` to the right hand side of the stage, using something like 24 pt `_sans`. Convert this to a graphic symbol, and call it `text`.

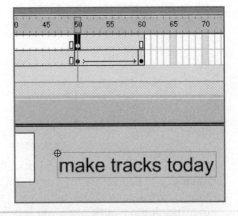

11. Position the symbol so that it lines up with the bottom of the stage (create a guide if it helps). Create another keyframe in frame 55 of the `text` layer, and drag the text across to the left so that it sits at the bottom right of the stage. Add a motion tween between frames 50 and 55.

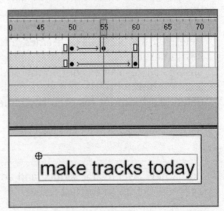

12. We're going to follow exactly the same process to bring a copy of the logo in. Add another layer, call it `logo`, and add a keyframe to frame 55. When you imported `logo_complete`, Flash should have included the whole `logo bits` folder in your library. Drag an instance of `logo_text` in from this, and place it just above the top left of the stage.

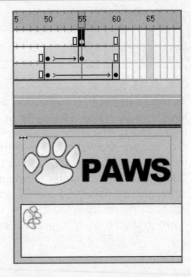

13. Add another keyframe at frame 60, move `logo_text` vertically down so that it fits snugly on the stage, and add a motion tween.

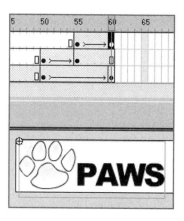

14. We're almost there – just a couple of issues to take care of. First, if you've tested your movie at all, you'll see it play nicely, and then loop around... and then everything goes a little bit wrong. Create a new layer, call it `scripts`, add a keyframe in frame 60, and add a `stop();` action to it. Test your movie, and everything should work well.

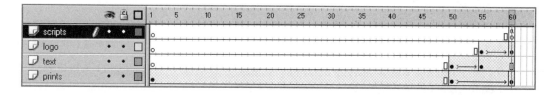

15. Finally, add another layer, and call it `btn`. Select the first frame, and draw a strokeless rectangle the exact size of the stage. We're going to turn this into an invisible button, so anyone can click on the animation and be taken straight to the PAWS site. Convert the rectangle to a button called `invisBtn`, double-click on it to edit it, and drag the `Up` keyframe across to the `Hit` keyframe. Return to the main timeline, and you should see that your button has turned cyan to show that Flash knows it's an invisible button.

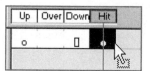

panel. Enter the following code, replacing the URL with the appropriate one for your uploaded site.

```
on(press) {

getURL("http://www.paws.com", "_blank");

}
```

17. Publish the file, making sure you generate an HTML file as well as a SWF. Upload the SWF to your server as we did with our other files earlier. We don't need to upload the HTML file as well - we'll be using the HTML code in our mail program to reference the SWF on the server.

> *We're going to use Outlook for the purposes of demonstration here. Other mail programs also allow you to do exactly the same, though – just search the help files for information on adding HTML into email.*

18. Open the HTML file you've just created in a text editor. Use the Replace, or Find and Replace option to find every occurrence of advert.swf, and change it (amending the URL as appropriate) to: http://www.paws.com/advert.swf

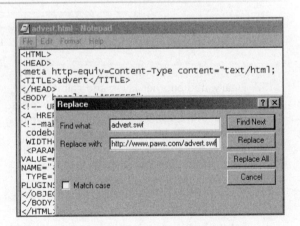

19. Copy the amended HTML file into Outlook's Microsoft Shared\Stationery directory. Unless you've changed it, or have several hard drives, you should find this under c:\program files\common files.

20. Launch Outlook, and go to Tools > Options. Select the Mail Format tab at the top, and select the Stationery Picker option from the Stationery and Fonts section. There will be a quick pause whilst Outlook searches for available stationery, and then you should be able to choose your advert file. You've now got a Flash sig file. Not all mail systems will display this properly, so don't assume that everyone who gets a mail from you will be able to see it, but anyone who can see it will be able to click on it and have the PAWS site immediately load up in their browser.

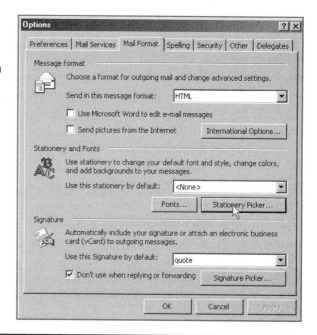

Monitoring

Once your site is up and running, and people are visiting, it can help to find out who is visiting it, so that you've got an idea of who to aim things at, and whether you need to create new content to bring different groups of people to the site. For example, you could check to see how many people were arriving at the site because they clicked on your email sig file, or you could keep an eye out for when the number of visitors started to decrease so that you could add a few more features to keep people coming back.

The easiest way to do this is to add a stats tracking system to your site. We are going to add the free and simple **extreme tracking** device to our site, but there are many other alternatives.

1. Open your web browser, go to http://www.extreme-dm.com/tracking, and select the `get free tracker` option. Fill out the simple form that follows.

2. Shortly after, you'll receive an email with instructions and a URL. Select the NO FRAMES option as shown, and the site will generate some HTML for you. Copy this HTML.

Choose the right trackercode for your specific needs:

Click here if you use NO FRAMES on your site and want to place the tracker OUTSIDE ANY TABLE.

Click here if you want to place the tracker IN A TABLE.
After placing the code, execute the following:
Change 'white' in the first line to the color of your background, e.g. 8500FF or NAVY.

Click here if you use FRAMES on your site.

Click here if you use FRAMES on your site and want to place the tracker IN A TABLE.
After placing the code, execute the following:
Change 'white' in the first line to the color of your background, e.g. 8500FF or NAVY.

3. Open `index.html` in Notepad or Simple Text as before. Just before the `</body>` tag right at the bottom, add a couple of carriage returns, and paste the HTML in there.

```
<A NAME=about></A>
<A NAME=contact></A>

<a target="_top" href="http://t.e>
<img src="http://u1.extreme-dm.con
EXs=screen;EXw=EXs.width;navigator
language="javascript"><!-- EXd=do<
src=\"http://t0.extreme-dm.com", '
height=1 width=1>");//--> </scrip
alt="" src="http://t0.extreme-dm.<

</BODY>
</HTML>
```

4. Between the HTML you've just added and the `<a name=contact></a>` tags, enter a `<br />` tag to create a slight gap between the SWF and the tracker when they appear on screen.

```
<A NAME=contact></A

<br />

<a target="_top" hr
```

5. Save the HTML file, and then double-click it to load it up in your browser. You should see a black image appear at the bottom: that's the tracking device. Click on it, and it'll take you through to the reporting page, allowing you to find out all sorts of details about your site visitors. (You should also be given a link to visit to find out this information in the email.)

6.   Upload the altered `index.html` file to your
     server.

Final steps

You've now created a finished website in Flash that makes use of all that Flash has to offer: animation, sound, video, ActionScript. Because we've shown you all this practically as we've gone through rather than waste words trying to describe what happens, we've covered far more than many other books would.

You're now a proficient Flash designer, but we hope you won't stop here. It only gets more exciting and more fun from here on in, and there are many, many ways in which you can take this further. This starts with the next section. There will come a time when you need to refresh your site and change it a little bit to keep visitors coming back, and the next section shows you how we approached this with the PAWS site.

Perhaps most importantly, when you start creating sites with powerful tools like Flash, the potential is so great that you can sometimes struggle to come up with new ways of using them. The bonus chapter that we've included on the CD gives you a few hints at how to approach the process of coming up with the ideas that feed great Flash design.

Beyond this, there are many directions in which you can travel, and friends of ED is here to help as much as possible along that journey. You could carry on to learn more about the power of ActionScript - it's really not as scary as some people make out, as we've seen in this book. You could spend some more time delving into Flash's sound and video capabilities, or you could get more involved in creating sophisticated animation sequences – it's no accident that many professional cartoonists are now using Flash.

Going even further, we've seen how to bring a text file into Flash, but combining Flash with scripts that run on the server, rather than in the Flash movie allows for some incredible functionality about loading other content into Flash. For example, you could design a site where users could customize the site to play their choice of music, appear in their favorite color, and so on. This sort of design is called **dynamic content**, and uses technologies like PHP, ASP, and ColdFusion alongside Flash.

Finally, there's also the prospect of creating 3d material for Flash with software like Swift 3d, and the exciting potential of Macromedia's Communication Server – which allows for real time audio, video, and messaging between Flash users. Whichever way you choose to travel, drop into the forum and let us know what you're doing, and how it's going.

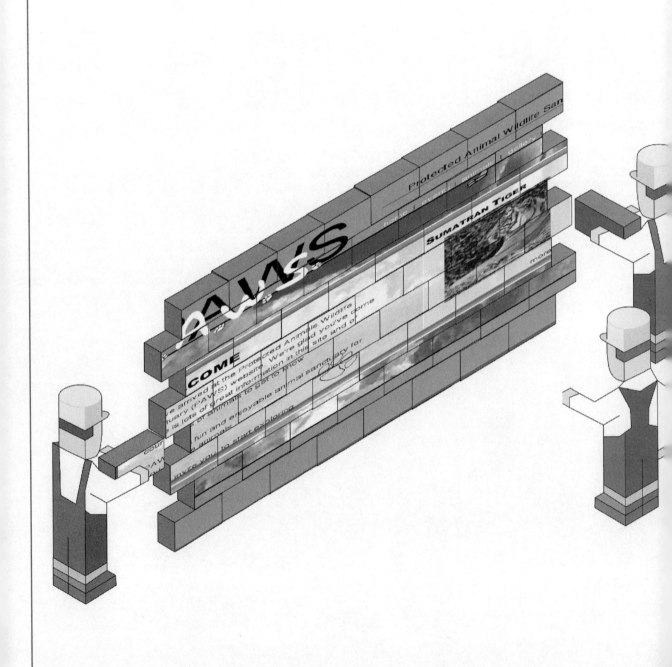

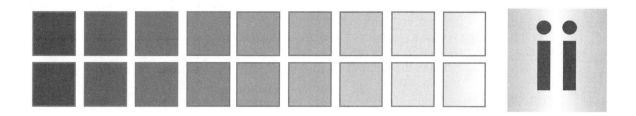

Adapting your website

The PAWS site that we've been building through the course of the book may be complete, but there are a few areas that we can tweak to make the site even more impressive. In this chapter, we'll start with what we've done so far and take it just that little step further. Planning a project thoroughly from the outset should hopefully prevent the need for major changes at this stage, but inevitably minor problems will arise, or a client will change their mind, or you will suddenly be hit by a brilliant idea that just has to go into your site. In this chapter, we will look at which last minute changes are feasible and easy to implement, and which ones are best avoided. We will also look at how best to make these changes in your Flash file.

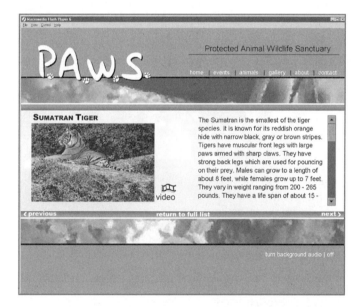

Open `paws_master_2.swf` to see the results of the changes presented in this chapter, then read on to see how we go about making these changes.

Enhancing the color scheme

There is something to be said for a lot of breathing space on a page. It gives the user's eye a rest, while focusing their attention on the content. Sometimes, though, white might be too bright a color (if you classify it as such) to use for that empty space. I decided to alter the background color of the site, and in so doing add another color to the site's color scheme. To complement the desaturated orange of the site's background image `red_02`, I chose a desaturated blue, `#6D99AD`, for the background color.

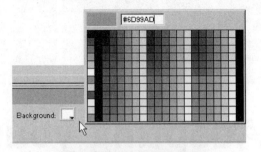

1. Open up the main file, `paws_master.fla`, and with nothing selected on the stage, click on the Background chip in the Property inspector. A small color palette will then open, type `#6D99AD` in this text field. This did wonders for reducing the feel of blank areas, without actually requiring any additional content.

Be careful when adding new color to your site, avoid garish color contrasts, and also bear in mind whether or not you will render some parts of the site unreadable by changing the color. Aim to make your site user-friendly at all times

With the new color added, I felt it would be appropriate to alter some of the supporting graphics to add some continuity and high lights. First, I chose to change the skin of the scrollbar component.

Any component that you get from Macromedia (like the scrollbar) can be skinned to fit whatever graphic look you need for your project. There are several methods you can use to do this. You can use code to change color properties of components, you can register new graphics for the components (again, through code), or you can directly change the color or graphics of a component's elements. The last method is probably the easiest, and most intuitive, if you want it to affect all instances of the component, so that's the one I usually choose.

2. Open up your Library in your main file, `paws_master.fla`, and find the `Flash UI Components` folder. Inside this folder you should find a `Component Skins` folder, and inside that should be an `FscrollBar Skins` folder.

3. Go into each movie clip in this folder (by double-clicking it), and alter the color of its graphics.

4. Select each part of the movie clip and adjust its color in turn. With each individual element selected on the stage, go to the Color field in the Property inspector and select Tint. You can then either enter an RGB value in the appropriate boxes, or click on the color chip to bring up a small color mixer.

Choose whatever colors you wish when you are changing the skin, but be aware that your changes will affect every instance of that particular component. In this case, that is exactly what we want.

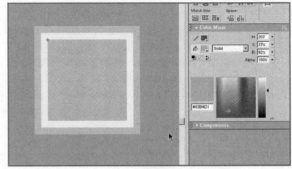

For my scrollbar, I used colors based on my new background color, using the color mixer palette to create darker and lighter tints, which I then applied to the scrollbar elements. You can create tints of a color by first using the Eyedropper tool in your toolbox to select a color, then selecting the HSB sliders in your color mixer (the drop-down menu at the upper right of the color mixer palette offers the option of HSB). The B percentage stands for brightness, so adjusting the value of this percentage will lighten or darken the selected color, creating tints.

5.   Once you have changed the colors of the scrollbar skin in the main movie, you'll need to go into `animal_content.fla`, and change the colors for the scrollbar there as well. Unfortunately, the nature of the component doesn't allow you to simply drag and drop your changed skin into the other movies, so you'll have to manually recolor all of the elements in each movie. As you develop further with Flash, you will learn about creating Shared Libraries that contain symbols you can use in multiple movies.

Shared Libraries work in a broadly similar way to Style Sheets, which you may have used in the past. Using a Shared Library would mean that you would only have to change the skin in a single file and it would update across movies. It's a handy feature!

6. To finish off the color enhancement, I chose to recolor the horizontal bar that was used in the navigation in the `animals` and `gallery` sections. Originally, it was colored with a black and white gradient, so all I did was add in a blue hue that matched the background to bring it all together.

In `gallery_content.fla`, go into the `base_nav` movie clip and alter the gradient of the navigation bar to (left to right) #496575, #8AA0AD, and #506F80. This keeps the same linear gradient, but makes it tints of blue.

7. I also decided to remove the tweening animation of the bar to tidy things up (we are going to add section transitions in a few pages). Remove the tween by selecting all of the movie clip layers' frames 1 through 4 and hitting SHIFT+F5. This will leave a single frame movie clip without a tweened animation.

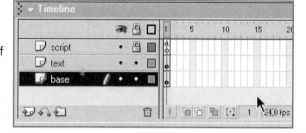

8. After seeing the blue bar, I thought it might be nice to drag a copy up to the top of the stage to border both sides of the content. Drag the blue navigation bar graphic (not the text) to the top of the stage while holding down the ALT key to create a copy. Use your Free Transform tool to rotate the copied bar by 180 degrees so that the gradient is in the opposite direction. (Alternatively, use Modify > Transform > Flip Vertical.)

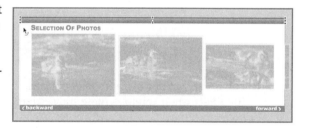

9. Test the changes you have made in the files so far by first publishing the gallery movie, then the main movie. Not bad!

10. I liked the double bar look so much that I actually added it to all of the other loaded content files. To do this, copy the two blue bars from the gallery movie, go into each of the remaining content movies and paste the bars onto the stage in the appropriate frames (the frames with the content, not the frames with the preloader). You might make an additional layer for the bars to keep things tidy. Also, you may have to adjust some of the content elements in the movies so that they are not blocked by the bars, or seem to be crowded by the bars - use your discretion.

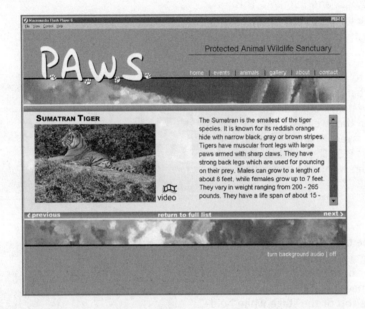

11. Publish all of the content movies and test the effect when you load these movies into your main movie. I think the border bars make a nice addition!

Fixing the navigation

The alteration to the background color requires some adjustment for the colors of our main navigation bar. As it stands now, the gray state of the navigation buttons is illegible on the blue background. Before we touch that, though, let's take care of the redundancy of the buttons. Currently, we have all navigation buttons in frames 15 through 40, and all navigation buttons but the home button in frames 10 through 14. I thought it might be nice to keep the navigation consistent for all sections.

1. Click frame 15 of the navBtns layer once. After waiting a second, click frame 15 again to select it, then drag the selected frame and drop it at frame 10 on the same layer.

This effectively overwrites the current con,tent on frame 10 and keeps the navigation buttons consistent from frames 15 through 40.

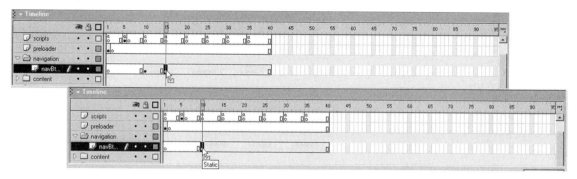

2. Double-click on each navigation button to enter symbol-editing mode for that button. Change the font color in the Up state of each button from gray to white. Do this by selecting the text field in the Up frame, then clicking on the color chip that appears in the Property inspector. Select the white color swatch from the color palette that opens up.

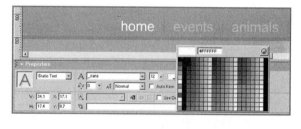

3. Now that the buttons are more visible for the user, let's add some functionality to keep users from clicking on a button for a section they are already in. Basically, if they are currently viewing the gallery, clicking on the gallery button in the navigation shouldn't reload the gallery. Just a little code takes care of this. On the main timeline, select the home button in the navigation folder and hit F9 to open the Actions panel.

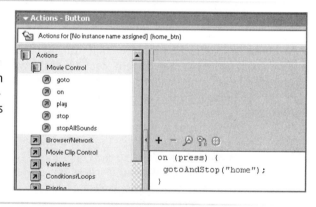

4. Select Expert Mode, by clicking on the View Options icon in the top right-hand corner of the Actions panel, and then choosing Expert from the drop-down menu.

5. At the moment, you will see the following code attached to this button:

```
on (press) {
      gotoAndStop("home");
}
```

6. Now type in the following lines of code to replace this:

```
on (press) {
      if (section != "home") {
            section = "home";
            gotoAndStop("home");
      }
}
```

Instead of the single `gotoAndStop("home");` that was there before, we have added a simple conditional statement to check if we are already in that section. Let's look at the code we have added in a little more detail:

The `!` symbol means NOT, so the if statement written in plain English translates to: *If the current section is NOT home, then proceed.*

`section` is a variable that will hold the name of our current section. This will change depending on the last navigation button the user has clicked.

What happens if the current section is not equal to `"home"`? Well, the section variable is given the value of `"home"` and then sent to that frame. If the user clicks this button a second time while they are still in the home section, then the `gotoAndStop()` won't run, since the section variable now holds the value of `"home"`, and will continue to do so until another section has been visited.

7. Select each remaining navigation button and adjust its code to match the code listed above, altering the string name to match the section. For instance, the code for the events button should read:

```
on (press) {
    if (section != "events") {
        section = "events";
        gotoAndStop("events");
    }
}
```

8. Similarly, the code for the about button should read:

```
on (press) {
    if (section != "about") {
        section = "about";
        gotoAndStop("about");
    }
}
```

9. Finally, when the user first arrives at the site, we need to set the section variable to "home" to begin with. We can do this in the scripts layer in frame 5. Add the single bold line to the existing script:

```
loadMovie("audio.swf", 100);
loadMovie("random_effects.swf",
➥"random");
section = "home";
```

10. That takes care of the new navigation, but if you publish and test your movies, you'll see that the same changes we made to our navigation need to be applied to the audio controls as well. In the audio.fla file, change the font color of the text in the Up state of the audio button to white, just as you did with the navigation buttons in the main movie.

That takes care of it. Now all the colors are working together nicely with our blue background!

Altering the logo

One change that would be easy to incorporate would be alterations to the PAWS logo. I decided to make something a little bit more playful than the blocky Arial lettering. You don't have to make the same changes as me - this exercise will show how simple it is to change the lettering to whatever you might need.

1. Double-click the logo on the stage of the main movie to enter its symbol-editing mode.

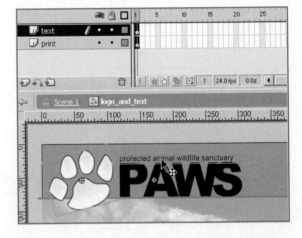

2. Delete the paw graphic on the print layer, and delete the text field containing the `protected animal wildlife sanctu-ary` text.

3. Select the text field containing the word *PAWS* and change its font in the Property inspector to a font of your own choice. I chose Hodge's Hand font, which is a favorite of mine. Make the text color white and change the character spacing from −10 to 10. We want extra space between the letters to put in punctuation for the abbreviation.

4. Drag an instance of the `logo_solid` symbol from the Library (in the `Logo bits` folder) onto the `print` layer. It will be huge, so use the Free Transform tool (or the Transform panel) to reduce its scale to about 2%. Place the paw after the letter P, where you might place a period or full stop.

5. With the `logo_solid` instance still selected, go to the Property inspector and select Brightness from the Color drop-down menu. Enter a percentage of 100 in the field that appears. This will make the paw white to match the letters.

6. Copy and paste three additional instances of the small white paw and place the copies after the remaining letters of PAWS. To do this, you can use the Edit menu to copy and paste, or you could drag and drop copies by holding down ALT.

7. Once all of the paws are placed, slightly rotate each paw to offer variation.

8. To make the logo stand out a bit more against the desaturated blue background, let's give it a shadow. Select the PAWS text field and copy it (CTRL/CMD+C), then paste it in place (CTRL/CMD+SHIFT+V). This will place the copy directly on top of the original. With the copy still selected, change the text color to black.

9. We need to send the black text behind the white text, so use the keyboard shortcut CTRL/CMD+SHIFT+DOWN to do this (the menu alternative is Modify > Arrange > Send to alternative is Modify > Arrange > Send to Back). With the black text still selected, off-set it by using your DOWN and RIGHT arrow keys to set the black text slightly down and to the right of the white text, creating a shadow. For more precision in placing the offset shadow, zoom in closer.

10. Create shadows for the four paws in a similar manner. Instead of changing the text color to black, set the Brightness levels for the copied paws in the Property inspector to −100% to make them black.

11. That takes care of the logo. However, the likelihood of a user having the Hodge's Hand font installed on their computer is slim, so it's important that I break the text field apart into a shape before I publish the movie. This will keep the look consistent for all users. This is an important step, which will allow you to use fonts without worrying if your user will have the same font installed on their machine. Before you do this, remember to save a copy of this logo into your library or another file, because after it's been broken apart the logo will be uneditable as far as its text properties are concerned, although you will be able to edit the shapes and colors of the letters.

12. Select both the white and black PAWS text fields and use the shortcut CTRL/CMD+ B two times in a row to break the text apart. The first time you use the command, the text will be split into individual letters. The second time breaks the letters into graphic shapes.

13. The final step is adding a text field with `Protected Animal Wildlife Sanctuary` to the main stage. In frame 10 of the logo layer on the main timeline, place a text field with the text `Protected Animal Wildlife Sanctuary` above the navigation buttons at the upper right of the interface. Make the font `_sans`, the color black and the size 16. Manually align the text so that it is centered above the navigation buttons at the top of the stage.

14. Select the line tool in the toolbox. Set its color to black and its stroke width to 1 in the Property inspector, and then draw a line under the new text field.

That's it for the logo changes! These were my choices for alterations, but feel free to incorporate whatever changes you see fit (or leave the logo as is, if you wish). For instance, I lowered the logo slightly so that the text dropped a little below the top border of the content window.

As you can see, no matter how you choose to change static graphics like the logo, it is pretty easy to make these amends at a late stage in the process. Other changes, however, are not so easily implemented; we are about to find out.

Adding transitions

One thing that's wonderful about Flash, sites and sets them immediately apart from their HTML counterparts, is the ability to incorporate smooth transitions between pages. If a link is pressed in an HTML site, the new page (usually) loads right on top of the current page, destroying, as it were, the previous content and making for a harsh and abrupt transition. On the contrary, page transitions within a Flash site can be smoothly tweened and animated in many exciting and creative ways—pretty much whatever you as the designer can imagine.

For the PAWS site, I felt that a simple opening and closing of the white border lines we drew at the top and bottom of the content window might make a nice and simple page transition effect. The process to create this effect was easier to conceive than implement, but was still possible. Other methods of page transition are also feasible, but would require altering the method of loading in the sections, or a large amount of ActionScript.

To make transitions work for loaded content, it's often helpful (and sometimes necessary) to load all the content into the same frame or frames on the timeline, as opposed to spreading each section across separate frames, as we have done. That way, you can transition one section out while you transition another section in.

You could also utilize code and perhaps the new setMask() method in ActionScript to create dynamic masking for the sections. However, the way we have set up the PAWS timeline makes this difficult. Instead, I chose to tween a copy of the background image over the existing section to transition the section out, then tween the background image off of the new section as it was loaded in.

The process is rather convoluted due to the way Flash allows masking and the way we have structured our timeline, but all will become clear as we step through the tutorial. Look to the finished file paws_master_2.fla for reference, and the finished movie paws_master_2.swf to view the final effect.

Opening mask

1. In the paws_master file, select the home layer in the content folder, and then create a new layer folder by pressing the Insert Layer Folder button at the bottom of the timeline.

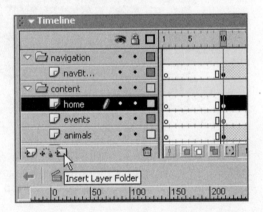

2. This should create a new folder inside the content folder. Rename the folder top mask.

3. Create two new layers and drag them into the new top mask folder. Name these layers, top to bottom, mask, and mask image. Create a keyframe for each of these new layers at frame 10.

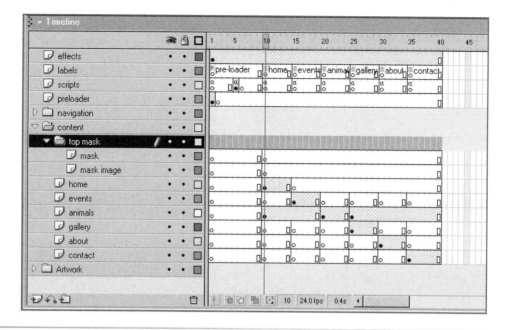

4. Select the `red_02` image that is on the
`red_02` layer in the `Artwork` folder (you
might have to unlock the layer to do so).
Copy it using CTRL/CMD+ C. Then select the
mask image layer you created in the previous step and paste the image in place using
CTRL/CMD+SHIFT+V.

It's imperative that this copied image is in
the same place as the background image,
as it should appear to the user that they are
one and the same. This is the way we are
going to fake the masking of sections to
create a transition.

5. Now that we have an image that will cover
the sections whenever we are transitioning,
we need to create the masks that will cover
and reveal this image during the transition
process. In the `mask` layer that you created
in step 3, draw a solid black rectangle using
the Rectangle tool in the Toolbar. The rectangle should extend from the very right of
the stage to the very left - the exact width
is unimportant as long as it covers the width
of the stage. The bottom of the rectangle

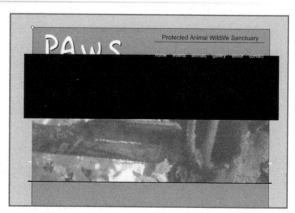

should be aligned with the middle of the stage, and extend to cover the top half of the content window (where we will be loading all of the sections). This will be the top half of the mask that opens up to reveal a new section.

6. With the black rectangle selected, hit F8 to turn it into a symbol. Make it a movie clip and set its registration point to be at the *bottom* of the movie clip. Name the new symbol maskOpen, as this will be the mask that opens to reveal a new section.

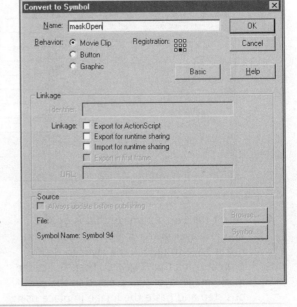

Now that we've created the main mask clip, we need to go inside it and tween the rectangle to make the animation. Then, we need to do the same for the bottom of the mask.

7. Double-click on the maskOpen instance to enter symbol-editing mode. Once in symbol editing mode, select the rectangle graphic and turn it into a movie clip by hitting F8 again (this will create a nested movie clip inside the maskOpen symbol). Name this new movie clip halfMaskOpen, and set its registration point as well at the bottom of the symbol.

8. Double-click on the halfMaskOpen instance to enter its symbol-editing mode. You now should be inside the halfMaskOpen instance, which is inside the maskOpen instance, and this, in turn, sits on the main timeline.

9. Create a second layer above the rectangle graphic and name it `code`. Name the layer with the rectangle graphic `rectangle`. With the second frame of the rectangle layer selected, hit F6 to create a new keyframe containing the rectangle. Then, add another keyframe on the rectangle layer at frame 5 as well. Finally, on frame 6 of both the rectangle and code layers, hit F7 to create a blank keyframe for both.

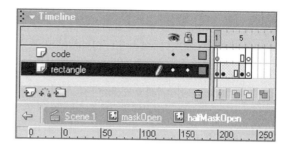

10. Select the rectangle at frame 5 and use your up arrow key to move it up above the content area that you can still see on the main timeline. This is where you wish the mask to open up to at the end of the transition. Then, with any of the `rectangle` layer's frames selected between frames 2 and 5, go to the Property inspector and select `Shape` from the `Tween:` drop-down list.

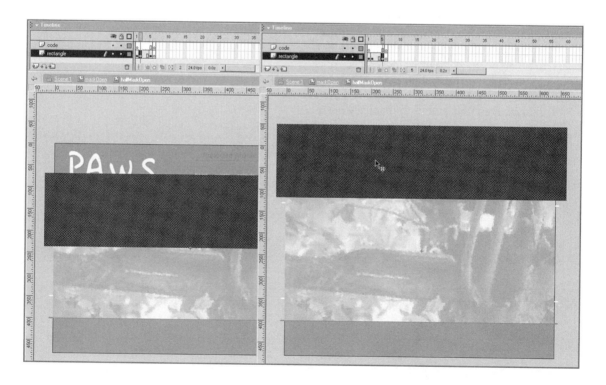

11. What we have now created is a black rectangle that remains static at the first frame, then tweens off of the content window in frames 2 through 5, and is removed at frame 6. Select frame 6 on the `code` layer and open the Actions window. Add a `stop();` action to this to keep the playhead at frame 6 after the tweening animation has played.

12. We have now completed the animation for half of our opening mask. The other half is a piece of cake, since it's simply another instance of this same movie clip! Go up one level in the edit symbol trail to the `maskOpen` symbol. Select the instance of the `halfMaskOpen`, copy it with CTRL/CMD+C, and then paste it in place with CTRL/CMD+SHIFT+V.

13. Keep the copy you have just made selected, and use Modify > Transform > Flip Vertical to flip the copied instance to cover the bottom half of the content window (this works if you kept the registration point at the bottom of the `halfMaskOpen` instance; if you did not, then you'll need to manually place the copied instance). See over.

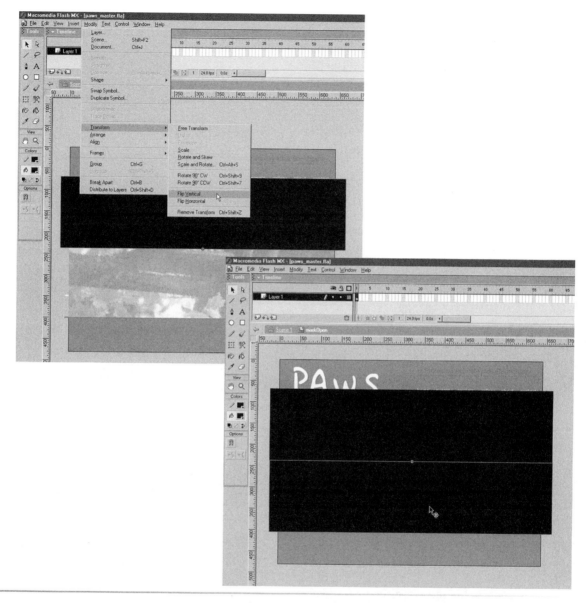

14. What we have now are two instances of `halfMaskOpen` - one for the top half of the content window, and one for the bottom half. These are both inside the symbol `maskOpen`, which will act as our mask transition for sections transitioning in. To allow for the extra time we need for the transitions, we need to add some space to our timeline. Expand every single folder on the main timeline, so you can see all layers.

15. Select frame 11 across all layers on the main timeline, and hit F5 a total of five times. This should add five additional frames to the timeline, and place the `event` label and its corresponding elements at frame 20 instead of frame 15. This gives us ten frames for the home section.

16. We need to repeat this process for all remaining sections. Select frame 21 across every layer, and hit F5 five times, then frame 31, 41, and 51 across every layer, and do the same thing. On frame 61, add 4 new frames so that the final frame on the main timeline is frame 69. This will make each section a total of 10 frames (0-9).

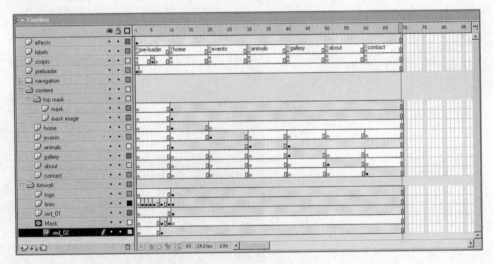

17. Now that we have extended the timeline, we can add a mask to the beginning of each section. In the mask layer that we added in step 1 (the layer that contains our `maskOpen` instance), create keyframes at 20, 30, 40, 50 and 60 by selecting the each frame and hitting F6.

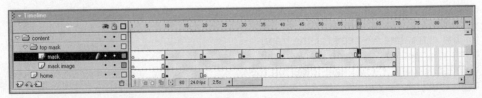

Closing mask

Now we have individual mask instances for the opening of each section. To make this work, we need to add closing masks to appear when a section is exited. We need to create these in a similar fashion to the way we created the `maskOpen` clips, but we can use the `maskOpen` symbol to help us out.

1. Open your library and select the `maskOpen` symbol. In the library drop-down menu from the upper right corner, select the `Duplicate` option and type in `maskClose` as the name for the new symbol. Then select the `halfMaskOpen` symbol in the library and duplicate it as well, naming the duplicate `halfMaskClose`. We now have duplicates to use for the closing mask effect.

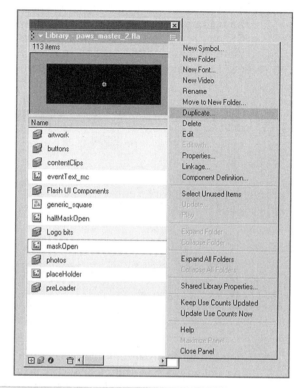

2. On the main timeline of the movie, add keyframes to the mask layer at frames 16, 26, 36, 46, 56, and 66 using F6. These frames will hold our `maskClose` instances, although now they contain instances of `maskOpen`. We'll fix that in the next step.

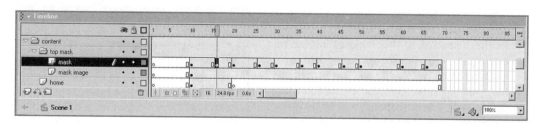

3. Select each `maskOpen` instance in each new keyframe you just created (16, 26, 36, 46, 56, 66). In the Property inspector, you will see a Swap button, which allows you to swap the symbol for another one. Click this button and a list of your movie's symbols opens up. Navigate to the `maskClose` symbol and hit OK. Again, do this for each new keyframe. We have swapped the symbols, but we still need to create the correct animation inside.

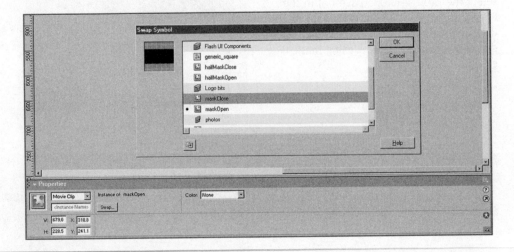

4. Select a single instance of the `maskClose` symbol on the stage and double-click it to enter symbol-editing mode. Once there, select both instances of the `halfMaskOpen` symbol and swap them with the `halfMaskClose` symbol you created in step 1. Again, use the Swap button in the Property inspector to accomplish this.

5. Now that we have successfully duplicated and swapped out the symbols, we need to fix the animation so that it closes instead of opens the mask. Double-click on the top instance of `halfMaskClose`. You should see the tweening animation you created in the last tutorial. The first thing you can do is delete the code layer in this symbol - we don't need it here. Instead, create a new layer and give it keyframes at frames 1 and 4.

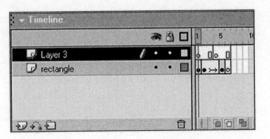

6. To reverse the animation, we are going to copy the rectangles from their ending positions and paste them into the new layer. Select the rectangle graphic at frame 5 of the currently tweened layer and copy it (CTRL/CMD+C). Then select frame 1 of the new layer and paste the rectangle in place (CTRL/CMD+SHIFT+V).

7. Next, select the rectangle at frame 1 of the currently tweened layer, copy it, then paste it in place in frame 4 of the new layer. This reverses the ending positions of the rectangle.

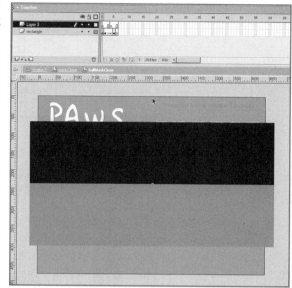

8. You can now delete the currently tweened layer completely by selecting it, and hitting the trash can icon in the timeline. You should be left with a single layer spanning six frames. We only need four, though, so select frames 5 and 6 and hit SHIFT+ F5 to delete them. Finally, select frame 1 and choose Shape from the Tween: menu in the Property inspector.

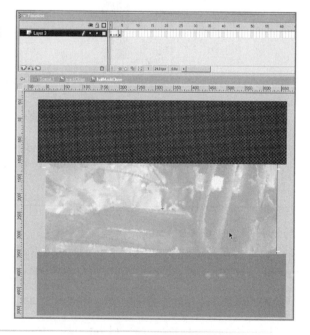

9. We need to let Flash know to treat our new tweened animations as masks. On the main timeline, right-click/CTRL-click on the new mask layer, and select the Mask option. This should lock your mask and mask image layers, which is fine since we won't be

touching those anymore.

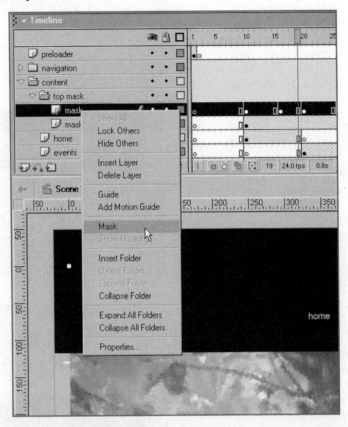

That's it, we have now created an opening and closing mask for our sections. Our work is not over yet, though. We need to adjust some code, and we need to edit our loaded sections slightly to accommodate the new transitions.

Navigation code

The way the navigation is set up at the moment, a button is pressed, the playhead is sent to a new frame, and new content is loaded. Our tweened masks will not work with this set up. First off, when a button is pressed, we want our mask to animate closed over the section content. We then need the timeline to be sent to its new frame, where new content is loaded and our mask opens to reveal it.

1. This is easily taken care of with just a few adjustments to our code. Let's look first at the code for the buttons themselves. As it stands now, the code for the home button reads:

```
on (press) {
    if (section != "home") {
        section = "home";
        gotoAndStop("home");
    }
}
```

Change the home button code to read:

```
on (press) {
    if (section != "home") {
        section = "home";
        play();
    }
}
```

2. All we have to do for each button is change `gotoAndStop` into a simple `play` action. Do that for each button in the navigation.

3. Next, we need to move our stop actions in our main timeline. We do not want the playhead to stop on the labeled frame, but instead stop on the frame where the opening mask has completed its animation, which will be 6 frames after the labeled frame (the opening animation, you'll remember, was six frames long, with the final frame being blank).

    Remove the `stop()` action from the scripts layer in frames 10, 20, 30, 40, 50 and 60. Add keyframes instead (using F6) on this same layer at frames 15, 25, 35, 45, 55 and 65. In each of these new frames, add a `stop()` action in the ActionScript editor.

4. Now we have the playhead entering a section and playing for six frames as the mask opens, stopping at the sixth frame. When the user presses a navigation button, the playhead is told to play, which sends it on as the closing mask animation plays. The last thing we need to take care of is the `gotoAndPlay()` action, after the closing mask has completed its animation and will

send the playhead to the proper section.

Create keyframes on the scripts layer at frames 19, 29, 39, 49, 59 and 69. In each of these keyframes, add the following code to the ActionScript editor:

```
gotoAndPlay(section);
```

5. One bit of clean up we should take care of here is that our logo is blocked during the mask tweening. To fix this, drag the `logo` layer up above the `navigation` folder in your layer structure. That's an easy fix!

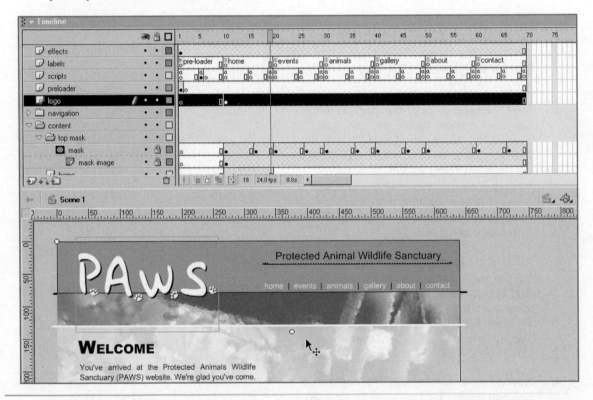

You'll be glad to know that that's all the code we need for our new masks to work. Let's step through the process again so you understand what will be happening behind the scenes after the user presses a button:

- First, the name of the new section will be saved into a variable called `section`.

- Then, the playhead is told to play, sending it through the animation of the closing mask before the new section is loaded.

- Once the closing mask animation is complete, the playhead is sent to the new section (thanks to the section variable), where the new content file is loaded and revealed through the opening mask animation.

- Six frames later, the opening mask animation is complete and the playhead is stopped.

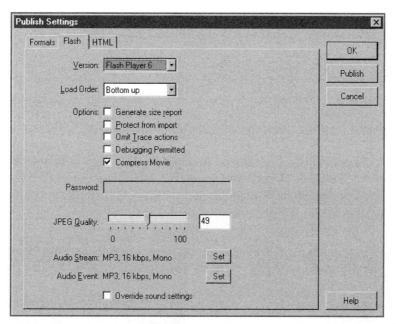

Go to File > Publish Settings in `paws_master.fla` and in the HTML tab, select Flash Only in the Template menu.

That's the transition effect completed. Test it out to see how it looks as sections smoothly transition in and out as the navigation buttons are pressed. To help the effect, I also chose to animate the white lines that border the mask. Look at the finished file `paws_master_2.fla` to see how you might achieve this effect as well (hint: it simply uses tweening of shapes—a process you should be very familiar with by now!).

Browser back button

The final element that needs a transition to be attached is the browser back button. We used named anchors to allow the use of the browser back button, but the inclusion of tweened transitions on the main timeline effectively breaks this feature. This is because when the back button is pressed, the playhead is sent directly to a frame and it automatically stops, therefore skipping both of our animated masks.

There are ways around this problem, but not with the configuration of our movie as it stands. This is a sage reminder of the importance of planning at the start of the process, and the limitations you will often face when it comes to modifying your site.

Adding gallery pop-ups

The final addition to the site, that I thought might be useful to incorporate, is in the gallery section. In many web galleries, users can click on smaller images to open a new window with a larger version of the same image. Since this is common gallery functionality, it made sense to include this with our gallery.

There are a few ways you could manage this for your projects. One very common method is to use the JavaScript scripting language to launch pop-up windows for the larger images. This is a little out of the scope of this book, so we are going to opt for the Flash alternative, which is easy and utilizes techniques you have already covered elsewhere in this book.

The idea is that you have each larger image embedded in its own SWF file. An invisible button over each image opens a new browser window containing an HTML page with the swf file embedded in it. The first things we will need to prepare are the files containing the larger images.

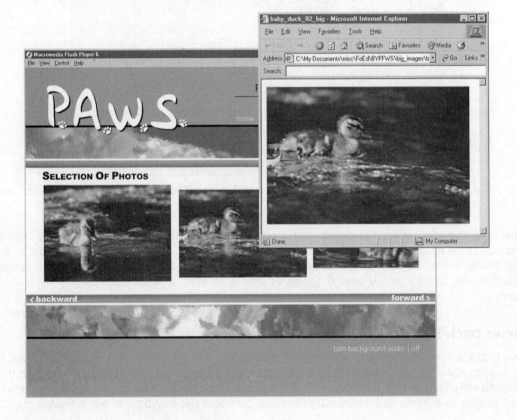

1. Create a new Flash file (File > New) and save it as baby_duck_01_big.fla into a new folder called big_images. This new folder should be in the same directory as your paws_master.fla file.

2. Use File > Import to import the JPG `baby_duck_01_big.jpg` [onto the stage. Select the imported image and look at the Property inspector to note its width and height (398x312).

3. Deselect the image, and with nothing selected on the stage you should see the movie properties listed in the Properties inspector. Click on the Size button and change the stage dimensions to match the size of the image (398x312).

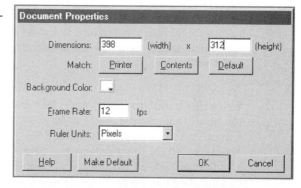

4. Finally, go to File > Publish Settings and make sure that HTML is selected (it should be by default). Go to the HTML tab and in the Scale drop-down menu, select the `No Scale` option. This will keep the Flash movie (and thus the JPG image) from scaling with the browser. Once you've done that, click the Publish button to create a SWF and HTML file.

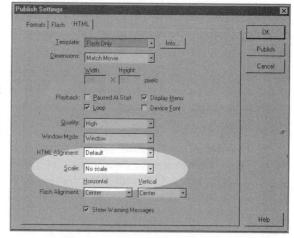

5. That's all that you need for the large image file. Now you just need to repeat the process for each remaining image that appears in the gallery. As you continue building with Flash, you will find other ways to accomplish the same thing in a more dynamic manner (for instance, using XML to store references to each image file and the new Flash MX feature of loading JPGs directly into a movie), but this method serves us well for what we have built.

6. The last step in order for the gallery pop-ups to work is to add buttons to the small gallery images to open these new files we have created. Perhaps you can already guess how we will do this! Open the file `gallery_content.fla`. The first thing we need is an invisible button. You created one earlier in the `animal_content` file. If you'd like, open up that file and drag the invisible button you already created into the gallery file. Otherwise, create a new invisible button in the gallery file.

7. We need a button for each image. Each button needs to be moved as the gallery moves, so it's important that the buttons are placed INSIDE the `gallery_mc` movie clip. Double-click on `gallery_mc` to enter its symbol-editing mode. Create a new layer named `buttons`, and on this layer drop an invisible button from your library over each image in the gallery.

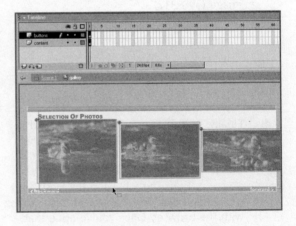

8. Now that we have buttons for each image, we need to add a little bit of code to open the larger image file once a button is pressed. Select the invisible button over the first image, which should be `baby_duck_01`. Open up your ActionScript editor and type the following code for the button:

```
on (release) {

    file = "big_images/baby_duck_01_big.html";

getURL(file, "_blank");
}
```

That shouldn't be anything too surprising for you now! The code needs to act on the button being released, so we use the handler on (release). The remaining code could actually be contained in one line:

```
on (release) {

getURL("big_images/baby_duck_01_big.html", "_blank");

}
```

I chose to split the line up to make it more readable and editable. I placed the file name for the larger image file into a variable called file. Then I used the getURL command to tell Flash to open that file into a new browser window ("_blank"). One simple command does it all!

9.   Use similar code for all of the remaining invisible buttons, simply altering the file-name to match the corresponding larger image.

10.   One final change I made to the gallery was to change the way the user controlled the left/right movement of the images. Instead of requiring the user to press on the forward and backward buttons in order to scroll, I decided to let the user's rollOver of the buttons control the scrolling. This is an easy change to incorporate. All you have to do is change the event in each button's handlers. Alter the backward buttons' code to read as follows - the changes that you need to make are in bold:

```
on (rollOver) {

_parent.gallery_mc.movingRight =
true;
}

on (rollOut, dragOut) {

_parent.gallery_mc.movingRight =
false;
}
```

See? Simply changing the event changes the functionality. Easy!

11. Now, publish this movie, then check out the new gallery when loaded into the main site. Clicking on images now opens larger versions of each image. That's a pretty nice addition!

Section adjustments

There are a few final small changes that will make things run the more smoothly. When a section is loaded the first time, we will see the preloader, but for all other times (after a section has been loaded once), the preloader shouldn't need to appear, even for a second. A few lines of code will take care of this problem.

In the preloader code at the start of each of the content movies (frame 1 of the scripts layer), add the following bold lines to the code:

```
preloader._visible = 0;
preLoader.onEnterFrame = function () {
            this._visible = 1;
            bytesLoaded = getBytesLoaded();
            bytesTotal = getBytesTotal();
```

These lines simply make the preloader invisible when it first loads. Then, if the content does actually need to be loaded and the enterFrame is run, it becomes visible. It's just a small touch to tidy things up.

Next, if you test your PAWS file, you'll notice that the two direct links to pages we've used cause problems with our transitions. Specifically, if you use the More button underneath some of the random animal pictures on the front page, or the Visit Us link on the about page, you'll see a white line across the middle of the page.

To avoid this, you'll need to move the content **and** script in both sections past the start of the mask, and place it before the mask starts to close again (we've used frames 35 and 65). You'll then need to add blank keyframes where the old frames were (that's frames 30 and 60), so that the previous section doesn't overstay it's welcome. Once you've done this, your timeline should look like this:

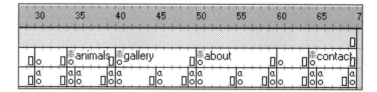

NB: When testing, we discovered a few issues with the scrollbars. If you use SWFs loaded into your main site, as we have, then only one of these should have a scrollbar component in it. Loading in two scroll bar components will cause conflicts, as Flash won't be able to tell the difference between them.

Flash will include everything in a movie's library – even if it isn't used – in a SWF, so if you have problems with your scrollbars, then check the libraries of your SWFs. In the case of the PAWS site, only `animal_content.fla` and the main PAWS file that we're loading it into should have scrollbar components listed in the library.

Summary

Throughout this section, we've made alterations to the PAWS site: some were large additions, while others were small tweaks. Altering the logo on a site will always be a fairly easy operation, as long as a new logo fits into the scheme of the site, but adding transitions is slightly tougher.

Thorough planning of your projects will help prevent major changes to your site at the end of the process, but tweaking is always inevitable – whether at the last minute, or at a later date when you give your site a facelift.

Keep your site structured and tidy with well-named symbols, folders, layers, and libraries, as well as clear and well-commented code, and this will make it a whole lot easier to make any changes. Plan and organize as much as you can, and you'll thank yourself for it later, I promise!

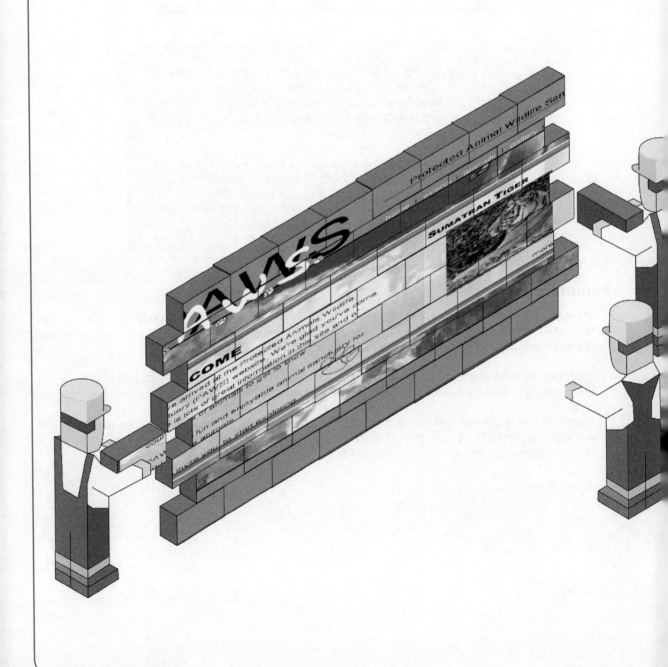

...archically, in alphabetical order, with symbols preceding the letter
...es also occur as first-level entries. This is to ensure that you will find
...e however you choose to search for it.

...welcomes feedback on the layout and structure of this index. If you
...ticisms, please contact: feedback@friendsofED.com

DESIGNER TO DESIGNER™

friends of ED writes books for you. Any suggestions, or ideas about how you want information given in your ideal book will be studied by our team.

Your comments are valued by friends of ED.

For technical support please contact support@friendsofed.com.

Freephone in USA	800.873.9769
Fax	312.893.8001
UK contact: Tel:	0121.258.8858
Fax:	0121.258.8868

Registration Code: 412734H7FEVZF301

Build Your First Website with Flash MX - Registration Card

Name ....

Address ....

City ....State/Region ....

Country ....Postcode/Zip ....

E-mail ....

Profession: design student ☐   freelance designer ☐

part of an agency ☐   inhouse designer ☐

other (please specify) ....

Age: Under 20 ☐ 20-25 ☐ 25-30 ☐ 30-40 ☐ over 40 ☐

Do you use: mac ☐ pc ☐ both ☐

How did you hear about this book?...

Book review (name)..

Advertisement (name) ....

Recommendation ....

Catalog ....

Other ....

Where did you buy this book? ....

Bookstore (name) ....City...................................

Computer Store (name)..

Mail Order..

Other..

How did you rate the overall content of this book?

Excellent ☐   Good ☐

Average ☐   Poor ☐

What applications/technologies do you intend to learn in the near future?..

....

What did you find most useful about this book? ....

....

What did you find the least useful about this book? ....

....

Please add any additional comments ....

....

What other subjects will you buy a computer book on soon?

....

....

What is the best computer book you have used this year?

....

Note: This information will only be used to keep you updated about new friends of ED titles and will not be used for any other purpose or passed to any other third party.

friendsof

D E S I G N E R   T O   D E S I G N E R™

NB. If you post the bounce back card below in the UK, please send it to:

friends of ED Ltd.,
30 Lincoln Road,
Olton,
Birmingham.
B27 6PA